Designing the Moment

Web Interface Design Concepts in Action

Robert Hoekman, Jr.

Designing the Moment:
Web Interface Design Concepts in Action

Robert Hoekman, Jr.

New Riders
1249 Eighth Street
Berkeley, CA 94710
510/524-2178
800/283-9444
510/524-2221 (fax)

Find us on the Web at: www.newriders.com
To report errors, please send a note to errata@peachpit.com

New Riders is an imprint of Peachpit, a division of Pearson Education
Copyright © 2008 by Robert Hoekman, Jr.

Editor: Wendy Sharp
Production Editor: Hilal Sala
Copyeditor: Jacqueline K. Aaron
Compositor: ICC Macmillan Inc.
Indexer: FireCrystal Communications
Cover design: Robert Hoekman, Jr.
Interior design: Joan Olson

ISBN-13: 978-0-321-53508-5
ISBN-10: 0-321-53508-1

9 8 7 6 5 4 3 2 1
Printed and bound in the United States of America

This book is dedicated to you, the hardworking designers and developers who have made it your mission to improve user experiences on the web.

Keep fighting the good fight. It's working.

Contents

Acknowledgments

A portion of my royalties from *Designing the Moment* will go towards offsetting the carbon footprint of the book's printing process, so you can enjoy the comforts of the printed word without worrying about damage to the environment.

For information on how I keep my company, Miskeeto, carbon neutral, please visit www.miskeeto.com/about/carbonneutral.

A great many thanks go to the following people, without whom this book would not be in your hands right now:

My editor, the amazing Wendy Sharp: You are the best in the business, and I'm proud to be associated with you. You make me better, sometimes in spite of myself, and I thank you for it.

My publisher, Nancy Ruenzel: Thank you for continuing to believe in and support my ideas and work, and for being receptive when I decide I need to fight for something.

My wife and best friend, Christine: For some unimaginable reason, you continue to put up with the long nights and weekends I spend glued to my desk while designing, writing, and running a business. I couldn't possibly ask for more. Thank you.

I also wish to thank the production staff at New Riders for all their brilliant work and dedication to this book. Special thanks to:

Jacqueline Aaron: Once again, you've made my work better with your diligence and attention to detail. Thank you.

Hilal Sala: Thanks, as always, for making things run so smoothly during the production process. You rock.

Just one more acknowledgment to go:

You
To everyone I have had the pleasure of meeting at industry events, online, and elsewhere since _Designing the Obvious_ was released, thank you. Connecting

with all of you is one of the best parts of my job. You've made every grueling flight, every long day, and every stressful weekend worth the effort. You've brought insights, questions, challenges, and even friends to my sessions, my inbox, and my social networks, and I am eternally grateful for your support. Thank you very much—I hope to see you again soon.

Author Biography

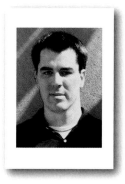

Robert Hoekman, Jr., is the founder of Miskeeto, a product development and web design consultancy focused on socially-conscious projects that improve the world.

He's a passionate and outspoken interaction designer, writer, and user-experience evangelist who has written dozens of articles and has worked with Adobe, Automattic, United Airlines, DoTheRightThing.com, Go Daddy Software, and countless others to create superior user experiences for a wide range of audiences. He also gives in-house training sessions and speaks regularly at industry events like Adobe MAX, Flashforward, SxSW, Future of Web Design, and others.

Robert is the author of the Amazon bestseller *Designing the Obvious*, which focuses on seven guiding principles of great web-based software and how to leverage them in any real-world project.

Introduction

A good user experience is all about good moments.

In one moment, a user's goal can be to figure out the name and purpose of a site after landing there from a Google search result. The goal of the next moment can be to figure out the controls for a video player to watch a screencast about an application. The next can be to figure out how to sign up, or to find out about pricing plans, or to contact the company.

These are not *life* goals, like those that many designers prefer to capture in the form of a "persona" (a description of an archetypal user within a particular product's audience), but rather *interaction goals*.

Achieving great design means asking ourselves, What is it we want the user to do in this moment and how does the interface encourage him do it?

What is the user's goal in this moment, and how does the design help her accomplish that goal? Is her goal to get oriented to a new site? Find specific information? Complete a form? Add something to the shopping cart?

Each moment has the potential to increase a user's confidence or destroy his trust in a product or company, and each one is an important piece of the whole experience.

Why? Because the task a person is attempting to complete at any given moment is the most important task to that person, at that moment.

It's our job to make sure nothing goes wrong. To make sure that moment is enjoyable and productive, and helps our user feel smart.

Our job is to solve for *all* of these moments. To design something that supports each of these goals without interfering with any of them. To create a cohesive whole out of the oft-disparate parts.

Our job is not to design screens, it's to design *moments.*

It doesn't matter how simple or complex an application might be. What matters is what happens when a user tries to accomplish his interaction goals for any given moment.

One of the keys to achieving great design is to look at our work in terms of what has to happen in each one of these moments to make it successful, and then solve for that.

▶ Navigating a Moment

In these moments, users take all kinds of actions. In the course of a day, they can cruise from Amazon to Z Gallerie and do everything from register to quit.

The actions users take online are broad and varied. We do things like input, edit, search, format, create, upload, delete, share, organize, and participate. These are the actions designers want users to take. And much of the time, these are actions we *want* to take.

Of course, we also do things we don't usually realize we're doing. We analyze. We judge. We forget, make mistakes, lose our train of thought, change our minds, get lost, and become confused. If we're lucky, we learn things. We get oriented. We form ideas, memorize, habituate, trust, get inspired, and feel productive.

This book is about designing interfaces that support all of these behaviors— you know, the things that make us human—in a way that is conducive to good decision-making in the moment a choice is presented. It's about creating interactions that inspire people to input, edit, search, share, and do all those other wonderful things we want them to do. It's about designing applications that help people feel productive in spite of their innate tendency to forget, make mistakes, and change their minds.

More specifically, it's a collection of over 30 stories that illustrate how to put good design principles to work on real-world Web application interfaces to make them obvious and compelling. From the first impression to the last, these stories are about looking critically at designs and questioning every detail to ensure that human beings—the kind that make mistakes and do things we don't expect—can walk away from our software feeling productive, respected, and smart.

Designing for the Moment is

- A revealing and insightful "think out loud" approach to interface design

- A critical look at elements from every phase of a user's interaction with a Web application, one moment at a time

- A set of best-practice recommendations for the design of everything from page layouts to social-networking features

Most of all, it's a critical look into the subtle details of an interface that make or break a user's experience during the moments he navigates his way through them, and how to improve each and every one.

▶ The Design of Interactions

This book is organized in order of the actions users typically take when they encounter a Web application, from the pivotal first few moments of getting oriented to the moment they finally close up their accounts and move on to something else. The titles of each part correspond directly to these actions. Each part is about something they actually *do* with a Web application in a given moment.

Parts 1 through 3 are about things users typically are able to do within the first 30 seconds or so of encountering a new application. The stories in these sections are about exploring an interface for the first time, finding their way around, reading bits of text to learn and get familiar, watching videos and animations, and searching for specific information.

Parts 4 through 6 are about things users do as they get more involved with an application. Once they decide to create an account, they input information, edit content, manage data, and participate in a variety of ways, and each of these moments can have a lasting impact on their confidence with an application.

And Part 7 focuses on what happens when users bail out, either temporarily or permanently.

In other words, I've intentionally structured this book so that it forms a complete picture of a user's experience with a Web application, in a way that addresses each and every phase of this human-to-product conversation, whether it lasts three seconds or two years. As a collection, the elements discussed in these stories comprise the complete picture of the online user experience.

The book is also organized in this way so that you can return to it later on and use it as a sort of "reference guide of inspiration". When grappling with the design of a new editing feature six months from now, you can open up the Participating section in this book, read a few pages, and hopefully get some ideas.

And it's all done via the timeless art of storytelling.

Postcards from the real world

Some of these stories are about specific implementations of design patterns. Some are about individual situations you may never face. Some are about new ideas. Some are about old ones. Regardless, they're all aimed at illuminating the thought processes, facts, findings, theories, and hunches that go into the design of great moments.

In *Designing the Obvious* (my previous book), I talked at length about seven core, guiding principles of Web application design that produce a common-sense approach that can be reproduced consistently and successfully in any Web project.

In *Designing the Moment*, I offer stories about how I've applied these ideas to real projects to create effective moments for users, and I offer a ton of new ideas along the way.

Some of these stories are personal—about things I've designed in the past. Some are brand-new, designed specifically for this book.

All of them are straight from the mind of someone who obsesses over the interaction design of, well, pretty much everything. Someone who lies awake at night thinking about how the local casual dining joint could tweak its drink counter to optimize the flow of customer traffic. Someone who spends the vast majority of his time thinking about the moments that make up a user experience and how to improve them.

Making decisions, out loud

At the end of *Designing the Obvious*, I talked about how important it is to step up and make design decisions, even if you're sure they will change later on. Regardless of how long each decision lasts, it needs to be made so that everything in a design is considered and deliberately directed. Nothing should be left to fate.

In this book, I attempt to do something I've never had to do before. I *articulate* the process of making those decisions.

I *think out loud* to try to shed some light on the *kaizen* ("continuous improvement") approach to design. To show how iteration is absolutely essential for achieving good results. To show how design principles, research, experience, hunches, and *feelings* are all applied to guide the design process.

In other words, I make decisions, out loud.

I also admit to mistakes, give credit to other people, and generally demonstrate that good design is the evolutionary result of a whole lot of bad design. Hopefully, through this, you'll see that good design is not merely the product of creative genius or moments of divine inspiration. It's the product of *forward momentum.*

You'll be able to go back over these pages for years and question my decisions. And you may reach a point where all the things I've said here have become ridiculously obvious to you, and you have surpassed anything I could offer you. My greatest hope is that this very thing happens for you.

I'm putting myself out there to try to help you learn to question yourself. To find fault in every design, and to continually look for ways to improve it.

Starting the conversation

With all that in mind, this book is *not* meant as a definitive guide for the design of Web interfaces. This book is offered as a conversation starter. It's meant to get you *thinking.*

These are not definitive answers, because there are no definitive answers. When I make a specific recommendation, it's based on my own experiences, perspectives, and knowledge. Sometimes, it's based entirely on my *hunches* (something every designer should have and trust).

As such, I can practically guarantee that you will come across something in this book that you think you can do better—some way to improve a moment for your users in a way I hadn't thought about. If you do, I want you to talk about it. Don't be an armchair designer—go out and tell people about your improvements.

Send me an email about your ideas. Blog about them. Tell your friends. Better yet, tell your coworkers. And your bosses.

I don't believe for a second that I'm the most knowledgeable designer on the planet and that everything I do is gold. I learn from and get inspired by other people *all the time*. With *Designing the Moment*, I hope to teach and inspire *you*, but I strongly believe and hope that you'll end up teaching others as a result.

If you have a good idea, talk about it. Keep the conversation going.

Everything we do can be done better, even when we've already done our best. I've tried to do my best with these designs. If you find a way to take them even further, speak up!

▶ And just so you don't need to take notes

Because typing out URLs found in books is a terribly annoying process of looking-typing-looking-and-typing-again, I've created an archive of all the Web sites, applications, blog posts, articles, research papers, and other stuff referenced throughout this book. You won't find URLs anywhere in these pages. If you want to check something out, visit **www.rhjr.net/dtm**. Click on the **Links from the book** link.

Without further ado, let's get to it.

PART I

Getting Oriented

There's nothing romantic about exploring the Web. We're not Lewis and Clark, packing up our lives and heading West to discover unknown parts of the Americas. No one dreams of discovering the hidden treasures of the Web, and there's not usually a significant reward for being brave and venturing out into the world beyond Google and our Web-mail applications.

Exploring the Web is usually purely utilitarian, like walking into a new store for the first time. Although we've seen a thousand stores in the past, the new one is bound to be a bit different than all the others, so we need to orient ourselves to the new environment.

Likewise, our job when we're on an unfamiliar Web page is to scan the page and try to figure out what the site is about, decide whether or not we want to stick around and check things out more thoroughly, and determine how to get around within this new space.

This process of becoming grounded is essential to our ability to feel confident and willing to explore things further.

As Web designers, then, our job is to help our users get grounded—and quickly. For this reason, the first several chapters of this book are about the things that happen within the first 30 seconds of visiting a site for the first time.

Within this tiny chunk of time, we need to accomplish several things:

- Present an appealing first impression
- Create clear pathways to information
- Offer tools to help the user get oriented
- Compel the explorer to become a customer

So in these first few stories, we'll take a look at everything from page layout to navigation, from search results to instructional screencasts, to see how all of these elements can help us accomplish our goals and help our users get up to speed with our applications.

1

Designing the First Impression

You know what they say about first impressions, right? That they can last a lifetime? Yeah, that's true on the Web as well. But not enough sites are designed with this in mind.

Steve Jobs, the fearless leader of Apple, is rumored to be obsessed with first impressions, which could explain why the first impressions of Apple products are always so gripping.

Opening up a new MacBook Pro, for example, is designed to make one's mouth water. First, the packaging creates a sense of anticipation and surprise. And once the box is open and the MacBook has found its way to your desk, the startup process is engaging from the first moment, welcoming you in several languages with a lively animation, detecting your Internet connection automatically, prompting you to port all your data and preferences from your previous Mac to the new one, and getting you set up against a backdrop of elegant imagery and attention to detail that makes the process feel effortless.

Translating this to the Web is not easy, but establishing an inviting and compelling page design is an essential part of our job.

Recently, a client who was working on a community site for graphic artists came to me with a boatload of requirements for a home-page design. He had already done the hard work of paring down his list of requirements to things that were all genuinely useful and relevant to the site's users. My job was to turn the list into a good first impression.

This home page needed a central area to highlight a large number of featured images, as well as smaller areas for high-level user account information, a featured item, and a way to sign up. Of course, it also needed the usual suspects—a logo, a tagline, navigation to other areas of the site, a Search box, and a footer.

And while all this seemed relatively manageable, the home page also needed to display headlines and snippets from articles about industry and site news.

The Featured Images section alone would take up a good chunk of the page, so figuring out how to add all the other items, *and* provide a section for news, was a bit tricky. After all, while these home-page features certainly did a great job of giving users what they wanted, the major *business* goal for the site was to get visitors to sign up and become community members. So I needed a design that drove users straight to the Sign Up Now button and made them want to click it.

▶ Discovering the Layout

I started by attempting to discover the layout, the most basic element of a page design.

I say *discover* because the layout of a page is not always up to the designer. When I think about page layouts, I often feel like the painter Bob Ross, who was famous for turning splotches of paint in his rich landscapes into "happy trees," always letting the painting tell *him* what to do next instead of the other way around.

See, you don't choose a page layout. It chooses *you.*

It's the result of the need to organize content, and it tends to take shape on its own. Once you gather up all the requirements for a page and get the content nailed down, your job becomes to *see* the page that needs to be created. Your job is to chip away at the block of plaster until the sculpture emerges.

To start my page grid, I did what I always do when tackling this essential and complicated piece of a design. Simply put, I threw a bunch of boxes onto the screen and moved them around to see how they fit together.

This process is a little like putting together a puzzle, but you're missing the picture on the box cover and all the pieces can be resized at will.

I gave priority to the Featured Images box, because it needed the largest area. I also created a nice, wide box for News, as it was going to need room for snippets of text. Things like My Account, Navigation, and the Featured Item got equal treatment in the left-hand sidebar.

After a few minutes, I had a first version.

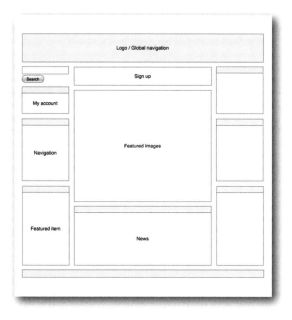

Surprisingly, the News section felt a little too wide. It enabled me to display long headlines and text snippets, but it also prevented me from clearly dividing the area into distinct sections of site-related news and industry-related news. To remedy this, I divided the section into two columns.

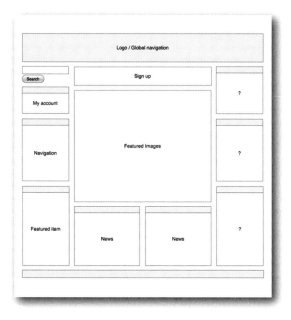

Better.

But then I realized something else. I had started this design by guessing that I would need three columns to accommodate all the requirements. Once I saw, however, that I had accounted for everything without the need for a third column, I removed it. Then I widened up the left-hand column to leave more breathing room for the Navigation and Featured Item areas. I also widened the boxes in the main content area, which gave me more room for featured images and news.

Now the page was starting to take shape. It was more focused on the main purpose of the site—to show off artwork from community members and relevant news—so I knew I was headed in the right direction. I moved on.

I knew that the primary business goal for the home page was to compel users to sign up, so I turned my attention to the sign-up area.

All that's usually needed in a sign-up area is some sort of call-to-action statement and a button. So I created some placeholder text and a button, and popped it into place.

Easy enough.

Now let me digress for a moment.

An 'Automattic' jump

Two weeks prior to starting this design, I taught a design workshop for Automattic and we talked talk about its popular blogging software, Word-Press. During this discussion, I worked with Automattic staffer Andy Skelton on a small change to the WordPress.com home page aimed at increasing conversion rates for the site.

We started with the original design.

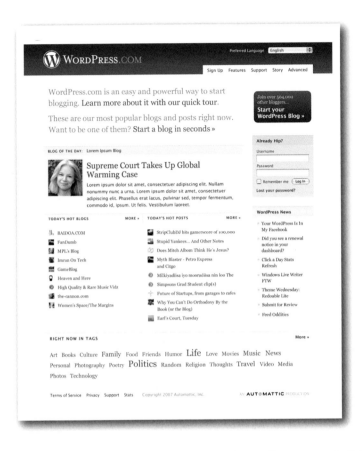

I created a wireframe version of the page (partially composed of clips of screen shots), and Andy and I discussed a few ideas for how to bring more attention to the sign-up area. I stripped out the blue box and replaced it with a big yellow banner area that contained a large Sign Up Now button. This not only brought more focus to the sign-up area, it created a clearer division between the sign-up area and the rest of the page.

From there, Matt Thomas, Automattic's visual designer and front-end code geek, created the final artwork for the page and started coding it up. The page was ready to go live a few hours later. (These guys don't waste any time at all!)

As he worked, we talked about changing the color of the Sign Up Now button to green so it would contrast with everything else on the page and stand out even more. He tried it out and it looked great, so he ran with it. Here's the result.

The grand total of what we did was increase the size of the sign-up area, write a call-to-action statement ("Express yourself. Start a blog."), and make the Sign Up Now button nice and large. We also made it green so it would stand out from everything else on the page. These changes helped to create a clear pathway to the registration page, which is exactly where we needed site visitors to go.

From what I'm told, Matt was the most optimistic about how much the site's conversion rate would increase as a result of the new design. He guessed conversions would go up 10 percent.

Turns out that this tiny design change made a bigger impact than anyone on the Automattic team expected.

On the first full day the new design was up, new blogs and member registrations went up roughly 12 percent and 14 percent, respectively. Cause for celebration. But that wasn't the end of it.

In the following weeks, conversion rates went up 25 percent and remained consistent.

This is a huge jump for such a tiny design change, especially considering that WordPress.com welcomes several million unique visitors every month. And if you've ever doubted that design work can make a difference to a project, well, doubt no more.

Because of this, I felt I could do a better job of guiding the user's eye to the sign-up area on this community site.

▶ Guiding the Eye

I noticed that if I moved the sign-up area beneath the Featured Images area, I could create what's known as "diagonal balance," a design pattern derived from the Gutenberg Diagram.

Applying the Gutenberg Diagram

In Western cultures, the eye tends to move from the upper-left to the bottom-right of a given layout, as though a page design has gravity. This is because Westerners read from left to right and from top to bottom, and the eye moves naturally in this downward path as a result. The Gutenberg Diagram simply illustrates this trend.

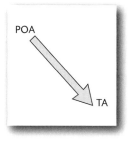

The top-left corner of a Gutenberg Diagram is the primary optical area (POA), and the bottom-right is the terminal anchor (TA). The top-right and bottom-left corners, conversely, are fallow points. Because a Westerner's eye moves naturally in this direction, layouts that support this diagonal balance are generally considered examples of good design.

The "diagonal balance" pattern is achieved simply by using visual elements to create an imaginary line for the eye to follow that moves diagonally from the upper-left to the bottom-right of a layout. The diagonal line is like an arrow pointing at whatever lies at the terminal anchor.

The animation sequence that plays when the Mini USA home-page loads, for example, even goes so far as to present each element of the animation in this order, following the diagonal line: First, the logo appears in the upper-left corner.

Then a rectangle is drawn out on the page, animating from the upper-left to the bottom-right.

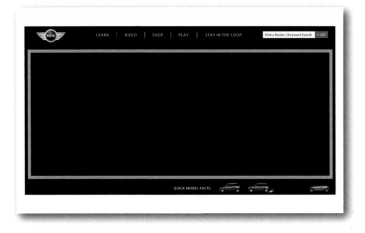

Finally, a sequence of Mini Cooper models slides onscreen at the bottom-right.

Dialog boxes also use this paradigm quite a bit.

Look familiar? Thought so.

To leverage the pattern on my client's home page, I reversed the positions of the sign-up and featured-images areas, creating a diagonal line from the site's logo to the Sign Up Now button.

To truly bring this to life, however, I needed color.

Use color to draw attention

Color is a fantastic way to draw the eye to specific elements as well, particularly when the color contrasts the other elements of a page. Human beings are hardwired to notice differences, not samenesses (is that a word?). So a little dab of color can go along way toward drawing the eye straight to very specific things on a page.

To accentuate the diagonal balance used on this home page, I applied the primary color from the logo—an ocean blue—to the Sign Up Now button. Then I used it as the background color for the Featured Images section.

I decided right then and there that nothing else on the page would be ocean blue.

With a unifying color to tie the three elements together, the user's eye is guided from the logo to a section filled with interesting and relevant content (Featured Images), and then to the Sign Up Now button.

So, having started with a simple layout that did nothing but accommodate the requirements for the page, I made tiny changes, one step at a time, to create a diagonal line that supports the natural tendency for Westerners to view a design from top-left to bottom-right. Supporting this natural eye movement meant the final design would help users become familiar with the purpose of the site more quickly and point them to what to do next, thereby making the page more approachable. In other words, the design helped to form a good first impression.

Diagonal balance won't work for every page design, so don't try to force it. But if you see an opportunity to accentuate the goal of the page through a diagonal balance, consider trying giving it a shot. And keep the idea of diagonal balance in mind when you begin a design to see if it lends itself to it in the first place.

For examples of several common page layouts, as well as some coded templates you can use to get started, check out the "Page Grids" section of the Yahoo! Design Pattern Library (remember, you can find all the links in this book at www.rhjr.net/dtm).

2

Showing Your Personality

I'm a minimalist. Always have been, always will be. In fact, I've often imagined that one day I would talk myself out of enough design elements that I would eventually end up creating a page with nothing on it.

Over the years, I've gone through more than a few designs for my own site, and each one of them has been only incrementally more or less minimal than the others. Back in my early days, though, I represented myself online with the most minimalist design I've ever put together. And when I stumbled across a backup of it recently, I instantly got all nostalgic about it.

The thing is, after several years of learning more and more about Web design and interaction design, refining my tastes, and honing my skills, I have yet to create another design that captures my personality better than this site I created so long ago. And you know, it always surprised me when I was complimented about the site, because at the time I didn't think there was anything special about it. It was so simple. So basic. So unglamorous.

See, the incredibly basic layout was nothing to write home about. And images were sparse, so there was really nothing to *look* at. And there was a lot of text on the site, so you had to read quite a bit. Overall, it was full of what I, at the time, considered flaws.

Turns out they weren't flaws. Turns out that the design communicated exactly what I wanted it to communicate—that I was a minimalist who loved to communicate in a minimalist fashion (ironic, isn't it?). This particular design revealed my *personality.*

All sites have a personality of some sort, but not all of them are designed that way intentionally. Some emerge by accident. When this happens, companies unconsciously risk letting any shade of internal strife affect its customer-facing touch point—the Web site. If a company has a morale issue, for example, designs can come out bland and uninspired. If employees are passionate and happy, however, designs can be exuberant, bright, and attractive.

The things I did to make this happen in my early design are things that can be done with any site to reveal the brand—the *message*—a company wants to communicate.

I didn't really know what I was doing at the time—I sort of just fumbled around with ideas until something stuck—but the extreme simplicity of the design led me to realize that the use of some very subtle elements to tie a design together can go a long way toward revealing the personality of an organization or individual. And it's usually a simple matter of accentuating what's already there to form a cohesive "brand."

Unifying a Design to Form a Positive Impression

When I started my design, I knew I needed a single-column layout because I had only a column of text and a single row of navigation items to work into the page. So I created a simple, centered column, just wide enough to show up on low-resolution monitors while still leaving a nice margin on either side.

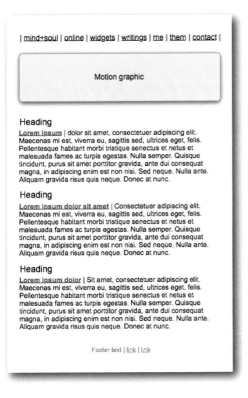

The top row was dedicated to the navigation items, and the space beneath it on the home page was reserved for a motion graphic. (At the time, I did a lot of motion design.)

Having left myself a wide margin on either side of the column of text, I decided to use the left-hand space for the brand mark. In this case, the mark was a very simple logo containing the words love and rage, divided by a plus sign (+)icon. This was inspired at the time by the movie poster for Baz Luhrmann's interpretation of Shakespeare's Romeo and Juliet. I know, I know—a movie as visually rich as that is a really obvious place to find inspiration, but hey, I was happy to have any inspiration at all.

Beneath this logo was a small, hand-drawn heart icon, which completed the mark. The "love and rage" idea, by the way, originated years before in a song I wrote (apparently, it's also the name of a movie). Again, happy to have inspiration, even if it was from my own arsenal of lyrics. This phrase has since disappeared entirely from my online identity.

I added the image to the wireframe and lined it up with the top edge of the motion graphic placeholder.

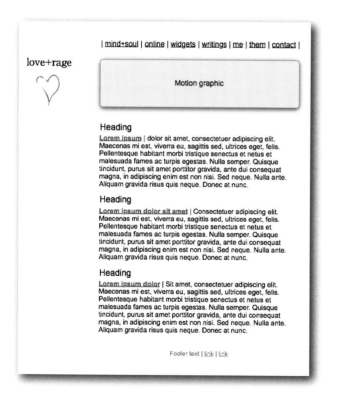

This was a good start, but it was definitely not enough to tie the design together. I wanted something that persisted throughout the site and unified each page to create a cohesive image for the site. What I needed was a character.

Using characters

I first learned about characters by watching movies. No, not those characters. The other ones. The ones that serve as metaphors and visual hooks throughout a film to represent a theme.

For example, the movie *In the Cut* (Pathe Productions, 2003) stuck to a consistently muted color palette, but occasionally inserted a crimson red that seemed to form a trail for the lead character (Frannie, played by Meg Ryan) from the beginning of her story to the end. The title of the movie, the story line, and a death scene were all inextricably linked by the color red. In essence, the color became another character in the film.

I learned more about characters like this from one of my personal heroes, designer Hillman Curtis.

When Hillman and his team designed the site for the film *Bend It Like Beckham* (Gurinder Chadha, 2002), they focused the site around a soccer-ball character that moved users from one section of the site to the next, unifying the design and maintaining the upbeat feeling conveyed in the movie.

Not all characters, however, are as dynamic and rich as the ones a cinematographer might use as part of a visual narrative. Most of the time, they're simple stylistic trends that permeate a site to thematically bring it all together.

In this case, I had a plus-sign icon and a heart. First, I tried the heart, figuring I'd use it alongside the headings on the page, like a bullet point.

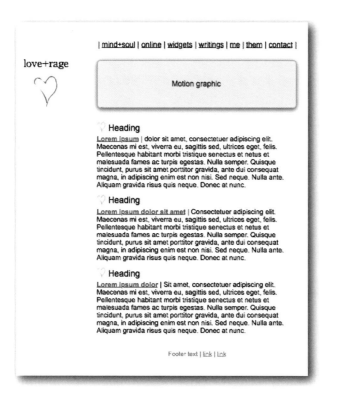

This seemed a little too, well, silly. I hadn't seen that many hearts in one place since I stopped passing notes in junior high school. This wasn't quite the image I wanted to portray online. So I scrapped the heart icons, and tried replacing them with a modified version of the plus-sign icon.

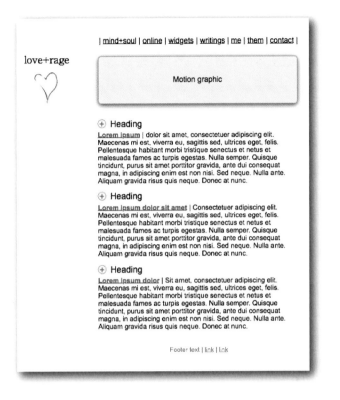

The plus-sign icon served double-duty. In addition to perpetuating an element of the logo through to the rest of the site, it also created the sense that each chunk of text on the page somehow rolled up into the heading, which was true. It also implied that the content was new, as though the "+" meant "just added."

OK, so I got lucky with that one. Luck is a big part of design. I never intended to reuse the element when I designed the logo. It just happened to work well, so I ran with it.

I noticed, though, that the most prominent text on the page—the logo and the headings—didn't match. And this inconsistency made me realize I needed to go one step further.

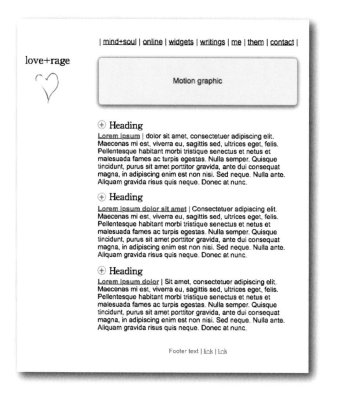

Instead of using HTML text to create the headings, I needed to use images, so that I could use the same font used in the logo. At the time I knew very little about accessibility or search-engine optimization techniques, and didn't realize that this was bad form. The matching fonts weren't an issue—it was the fact that sticking text into images meant that search-engine spiders couldn't read the headings, and that screen readers (for the visually impaired) couldn't either.

In my naiveté, I plowed forward. I coded up the page template, created my motion graphic, and built out all the pages for the site.

To maintain the character of the plus-sign icon, I used it on every page, for each heading. And since I had one other page with an "and" in the title, I used the icon there as well.

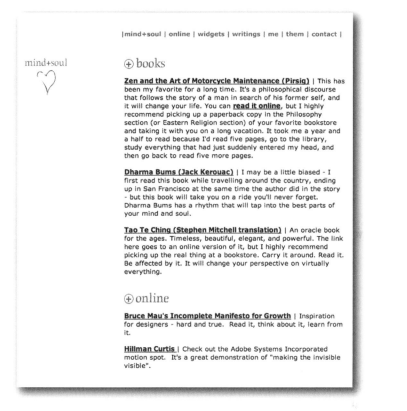

And there you have it. My simple, basic, unglamorous site, chock-full of flaws. The one I love more than any site I've designed for myself since.

One of these days, I hope to create a version of my site that captures my personality as well as this old design did. And next time, I hope I'm wise enough to realize that I love it.

As I've said, a site has a personality whether it's designed intentionally or not. By paying attention to what is being communicated, and making some relatively simple changes, we can reshape our image online any way we want. Odds are, most of us don't want to look bland and uninspired. Usually, we have a specific vibe we want to get across to users. Brand marks, and characters derived from brand marks, can bring that message to life in an elegant, approachable way, and show our users what we really want them to see.

That said, keep your brand marks subtle and elegant. We can't just toss up soccer balls and hope they fly. We need to temper our brand marks and characters with good judgment, and err on the side of simplicity.

3

Zen and the Art of Navigation

The key to being able to find your way around an application you're using for the first time is understanding how the site is structured, and these first few moments spent getting oriented are pivotal to a good first impression.

Confusing terminology and poor organization, though, can cause us to go from hopeful and interested to frustrated very quickly, so it's vitally important that we're able to find our way around quickly.

We often get oriented by glancing around a page to see what options exist and quickly filtering out things that don't apply. For example, when looking for information about a company, we look for the words *About, Company, Us,* and similar terms. When we see terms that *don't* fit what we want, we ignore them. When we see a term that *does* fit, we look more closely at the word and its immediate surroundings to see if something there is what we need. If it is, we click.

In other words, we look at major page sections for something relevant, then at items within sections for something *more* relevant, and eventually— *hopefully*—at the exact thing we're seeking (or, in a passive browsing mode, we look at something that is more interesting than everything else on the page).

This process of deduction doesn't just help us get oriented to a new site, it also helps us later on, after we've used the site for a while and need to find information or complete tasks again. For this reason, it's absolutely vital that navigation, well, *makes sense.* Not in a way that reflects the underlying system, but in a way that makes sense to *us.* The site has to support the way we think.

I was once tasked with redesigning a Web-based WYSIWYG (what you see is what you get) site-builder application. Like Google Page Creator, the application was meant to provide a way for users to create and edit a Web site using visual editing tools, eliminating the need to write code.

Unlike Page Creator, though, this application had existed for a long time and had gone through quite a few major revisions. As more and more features were added, the navigation for the site became more than a little cumbersome. New interface elements were sort of just tacked on wherever they could be, and it became increasingly difficult for users to figure out how to complete tasks.

It was a less than ideal situation for a Web application that tens of thousands of people were using to create their Web sites.

The development team and I worked together on a major overhaul of the application for several weeks. The navigation was just one small piece, but it was an important piece.

▶ Telling the Software What to Do

When I took on the job of reworking the site-wide (or persistent) navigation, it appeared fairly simple. It consisted of two buttons labeled Home and Site. But the Site button produced a menu that provided access to a wide variety of application functionality, and the menu items were in no particular order.

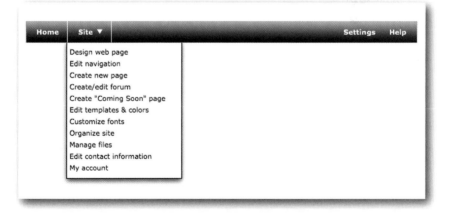

The real menu was actually quite a bit longer than the one shown here, but you get the idea. Each menu option led to a completely different task flow for a completely different reason. The "Create new page" and "Edit contact information" options, for example, had absolutely nothing to do with each other. No user would think to himself, I want to edit my contact information, so I'll look under the Site menu. But there the two options were, sitting next to each other like lost puppies.

These different types of actions could be grouped somewhat naturally. Looking down the list, I saw nouns that related to each other. Things like "Web page," "New page," and "navigation" were all site components that could be created and edited. "Templates and colors" and "fonts" related to the appearance of a Web site.

So I took a run at dividing the menu options into several groups that better reflected their natural relationships, and then labeling them. The new labels looked like this:

| Home | Site ▾ | Add-ons ▾ | Styles ▾ | Misc. ▾ | | Settings | Help |

These new labels split the original list of options into groups of site elements, add-on features (such as a forum), and style features. From there, I took a look at how each menu would look under its new heading. While doing this, I removed the verb from each menu option (edit, manage, and so on), leaving simpler terms that could be scanned quickly. Just run your eyes down the list and choose "Web page," "Navigation," or whatever you need.

| Home | Site ▾ | Add-ons ▾ | Styles ▾ | Misc. ▾ | | Settings | Help |

Web page
Navigation

| Home | Site ▾ | Add-ons ▾ | Styles ▾ | Misc. ▾ | | Settings | Help |

New page
Forum
Coming Soon page

| Home | Site ▾ | Add-ons ▾ | Styles ▾ | Misc. ▾ | | Settings | Help |

Templates & colors
Fonts

| Home | Site ▾ | Add-ons ▾ | Styles ▾ | Misc. ▾ | | Settings | Help |

Site organization
Files
Contact information
Account

The grouping seemed to make sense, but I ended up with a menu with only one option in it, and, as you can see, I'd also created a weird "junk drawer" menu called "Misc.".

Every app needs a junk drawer, right?

Yeah, I didn't like it either. It made sense for about five seconds, until I realized that I hated it. At first, I hated not having a better noun to represent the items under the Misc. menu. Then I realized that the lack of a good noun wasn't the problem.

Everybody wants to direct

See, software doesn't exist just so we can click buttons. It exists so we can accomplish tasks. So we can *do things*.

So navigation shouldn't be a bunch of nouns in a row of buttons. Navigation should help us feel like we're getting something done. It should also enable us to feel like we're in the driver's seat.

We human beings don't like to feel as if we have to do what the software wants us to do. In the moment when we decide to take action, we want to control the software. We want to tell *it* what to do, not the other way around. Software that goes against this inclination feels clunky and awful.

And if you look around, you notice that a lot of software navigation is designed to make us feel like we're in charge. Menus in everything from Microsoft Word to Adobe Illustrator include options to do things like Edit and View.

These menus are not object based. They're *task* based. The way they should be.

In my menus, I focused on and reorganized *objects* when I should have focused on the types of tasks that could be accomplished in the application. In doing this, the terminology would have come out as *verb-noun pairs* instead of just ugly old nouns.

Verb-noun pairs, as you might guess, are simply combinations of words that start with a verb and end with a noun. They're structured this way so that we can tell the software which action we want to take, and to what object we'd like the action to be applied. This enables us to feel like we're *directing* the software. Like we're the ones in charge.

Without the verbs, my menus were clunky and awful.

To remedy the situation, I changed the noun-driven button labels into verb-driven labels.

Instead of choosing Styles > Fonts for this task, you would now tell the software to "Manage Fonts." The button label was the verb, and the menu option was the noun.

Now users could feel in charge of the software. Now they could "Design" navigation or an existing Web page, "Create" a forum or a new page, and "Customize" the site organization, files, and so on.

(If the user was meant to choose a font for some text in a Web page, by the way, I'd advocate the use of Choose > Fonts, but in this case, the user was literally meant to manage the fonts available for use in site images, which could be customized to include text.)

I just needed to do one more thing before I handed it off to the development team.

Avoid Login syndrome

Every designer has pet peeves. The use of the term Login, and the inverse, Logout, is mine.

I've worked on many applications that used these terms, and seeing them in use always makes me wonder.

The people who conceive, design, and build Web applications have a lot of commitment. This stuff isn't easy. You have to be really devoted to the idea of building a great application to actually pull it off.

Developers, managers, designers, and so on spend countless hours planning, writing code, running usability tests, and everything else they can think of to create an application. Then, despite all this incredibly hard work, they leave the copy to, well, whoever happens to write it. And that person very often types up the word Login and leaves it at that.

Home   Blog   Learn   Signup*Free!*   Login

Member Login

Member Name:

jsmith

Password:

••••••••

Login

Login to RPM

PLEASE LOGIN:

Username: jsmith

Password: ••••••

Two of these images are from extremely well-known and reputable Web applications. And right there on the home page is a basic grammatical error. And it's one that every single member of the site is going to see and click at some point. Possibly as often as once a week, possibly every day.

In each of these and countless other examples all over the Web, the term login is used incorrectly.

Login is not an action, in the same way that shoe is not an action. It's a noun—as "the login interface."

You don't want users to "login." That makes no sense. You want users to log in. Using login in an application interface indicates a lack of professionalism. A lack of commitment to making sure that everything in your application was carefully considered and designed on purpose.

It's like sticking up a sign that says, "We care, but not 100 percent."

Plus, users don't want to interact with objects in interfaces—they want to do things. They don't want to click to see the Login widget. They want to log in.

It's not a noun you want. It's a command.

My project included the term Login.

So I changed it into a command.

Most people may never give a single conscious thought to whether this is displayed as one word or two. But even without conscious attention, the incorrect use of this term can make an application feel less professional. The difference is so simple, but so important. Ensuring that every last detail is correct communicates to users that

"I care. 100 percent. All the way."

Never ever stop caring at 99 percent. If you do, you lose an opportunity to do better. Everything is important.

Say what you do and do what I say

Our users' ability to find their way around a site, get the information they need, and complete tasks is key to maintaining interest in the site. By helping our users get around with a clear navigation structure, we enable them to see not only what the site can do, but how to do it.

In verb-noun pairs, buttons and links do an effective job of telling users what they can do, and also allow users to feel in control by telling the application what to do instead of the other way around.

When creating application navigation, be sure to support the way a user thinks and not how the system thinks. The user is not the tool. The system is the tool.

4

All Links Are Not Created Equal

No matter what news portal you use—whether it's BBC News, CNN, Yahoo, or some other page entirely—you face lists of links, sorted by time, relevance, popularity, or some other criteria. And this is a good thing, because it makes information relatively easy to find.

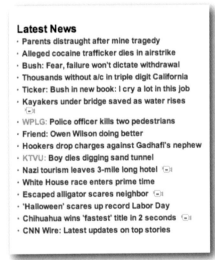

That said, even the most basic and standardized designs can be improved. Recently, while creating a list of links, I saw an opportunity to do just that.

In this particular case, the goal was to create a list of headline links for the home page of a corporate intranet that let call-center employees know about current issues. The links needed to appear in chronological order, like a news portal, but only five headlines needed to be shown at any one time.

I started with the usual suspect. I created a simple list of links.

Most recent headlines

Title of most recent story (...)
Title of slightly less recent story (...)
Title of slightly less recent story (...)
Title of slightly less recent story (...)
Title of slightly less recent story (...)

The next step was to determine how to communicate to users that the order of the links reflected the order in which the articles were posted. In this call center, the newest issue was always the most important.

To do this, I could have included a bit of instructive text that said something like, "Sorted from newest to oldest," but this would require more reading than most people bother to do in a Web application.

Instead, I numbered the headlines from one to five and considered calling it a day.

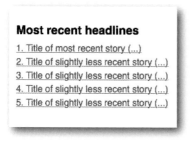

Most recent headlines

1. Title of most recent story (...)
2. Title of slightly less recent story (...)
3. Title of slightly less recent story (...)
4. Title of slightly less recent story (...)
5. Title of slightly less recent story (...)

Numbering the items was probably sufficient to communicate the order of the links. But it bothered me that these lists were still flat. Even though each item was numbered, each item still looked exactly like all the other items.

In this call center, the newest issue listed was usually incredibly important. It usually meant something happened elsewhere in the company that needed to be communicated to customers pronto. These headlines could be about service outages, temporary billing-system failures, or other things that required call-center employees to have up-to-the-minute information.

How was a flat list of links, where every link looked just like the other, going to communicate the importance of the No. 1 item?

Having recently read an article on Boxes and Arrows, called "Ambient Signifiers," by Ross Howard, I felt inspired to try something out.

▶ Using Ambient Signifiers As Navigational Clues

In the article, Howard explained that each station along the Japanese commuter-train route has its own chime melody associated with it (in addition to signs). The idea is that commuters who frequently take the same route—to and from work, for example—become bored and start reading books and newspapers or working on their laptops, but will learn to recognize the melody played at the station prior to their stop and begin preparing to get off the train.

Howard called these chimes **ambient signifiers**. Along with other ambient features of the commute, such as tunnels, the appearance of each station, and so on, these melodies help commuters build a mental map of their commute and avoid missing their stop.

The idea of ambient signifiers intrigued me because it meant that users could accomplish a task on a site almost subconsciously, and on this corporate intranet, the ability to find the right information that easily would be extremely helpful. So I tried applying the concept of ambient signifiers to my list of links.

I scrapped the numbering system and changed the font size for each link based on its age. I used the largest font for the link to the most recent article, and incrementally smaller font sizes for each link to articles as they got older and less important.

Most recent headlines

Title of most recent story (...)
Title of slightly less recent story (...)
Title of slightly less recent story (...)
Title of slightly less recent story (...)
Title of slightly less recent story (...)

This alone changed things quite a bit. The larger font stood out more than the smaller ones, making it relatively obvious that the first link in the list was more important than the others. Also, the larger font appeared darker and heavier, which made it stand out even more.

Showing signs of age on the Web

As I worked, I remembered something designer Brendan Dawes talked about in his book, *Analog In, Digital Out.* Dawes waxed nostalgic about an old brochure he'd come across for his first computer that had at some point acquired a tea stain, and talked about the lack of a sense of *age* in the digital realm. Digital files cannot acquire tea stains. And while this creates a major advantage for digital files over physical objects—they maintain their quality even years after being created—it also means the sense of nostalgia one can get over tea-stained physical objects is lost in the digital world.

This idea sent my little brain reeling, of course, because wow—just imagine all the design tricks you could use to imply age on a Web page!

It has actually always bothered me that the Web shows no sense of age—I just hadn't articulated the gnawing feeling that old things needed to somehow appear old. Yes, many Web pages display dates to indicate when they were originally posted, but since this is usually the only indication of age, it can easily be missed. And many Web pages have no date at all—nothing whatsoever to indicate age.

An article I wrote three years ago, for example, can very easily come up as a top search result today. And if no date accompanies the article, what's to stop someone from thinking it was just posted yesterday?

Hence, I get email occasionally from people who have questions about something I haven't thought about in three years. The question is fresh. My answer, however, might be a little rusty.

If the Web showed signs of age, however, the user reading the three-year-old article could clearly see that the article was old, and might therefore seek more updated information elsewhere, or at the very least, adjust his question to me.

Taking Brendan's idea to heart, I decided to take my link-list design a step further and try to communicate the *age* of each link. After all, in this case, newer meant more important.

But how do you make a link look old?

Google Reader had an answer for this one. A new version of the application happened to launch around the same time that I was working on this link list, and I had noticed a tag cloud in Reader that had a little extra depth than most (more on tag clouds in the next chapter). This one used color as well as font size to indicate the relative popularity of a link.

Tags
The more items a tag has, the bigger it appears. The more of those items you have read, the darker it is.

clients **general** gigs my-sites podcasts user-experience web-apps web-standards world-changing

It included instructive text that said, "The more items a tag has, the bigger it appears. The more of those items you have read, the darker it is."

I thought this was a bit wordy for instructive text, but I also thought the dual-indicators (size and color) were a great idea. So I rolled with it.

Modifying my link list, I changed the color of the links from dark to light as the list descended from newest to oldest.

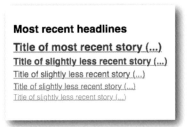

Most recent headlines
Title of most recent story (...)
Title of slightly less recent story (...)
Title of slightly less recent story (...)
Title of slightly less recent story (...)
Title of slightly less recent story (...)

This final adjustment created the sense that the links faded from new to old, and thus it became quite clear that the first link was the most important and that the links decreased in importance from there on.

Perfect. It was exactly what I had *no idea* I wanted.

Would this use of ambient signifiers make a major difference on the resulting Web page? Probably not. Would some people be annoyed by the tiny font used for the last link in the list? Possibly, but the font sizes could be adjusted so that this didn't happen. Am I saying you should immediately run out and do this on your own page?

Only if it makes sense.

The notion of ambient signifiers is almost completely untapped on the Web, and there are likely myriad ways it can be applied. So take a look around and see if the idea can be used to improve something in your own design. If you can help a user find the information he wants, in the moment he wants it, you're on to something.

Don't force it, but keep your eye out for opportunities. And keep your other eye out for inspiring ideas, even when they appear completely irrelevant to whatever you're working on. You never know when one of them will spark an idea for something new or an improvement over an old standard.

In this case, I was able to do something I think genuinely improved upon an old idea, but the point was really just to help users get oriented. Anything you can do to create clear pathways helps users. They should be able to glance around the page and *automatically* understand the meaning of the link order. It should be intuitive, not something that requires thought and examination.

5

Getting Your Head Out
of the Tag Cloud

In *Designing the Obvious*, I mentioned a time that a designer came to me with a design for the sidebar of a blog template that included a tag cloud. The design also included two buttons—one for displaying a cloud, the other for displaying a list.

I'd like to expand on that story a bit, because I've learned a few things since writing *Designing the Obvious* that have changed my perspective.

If you don't already know, a **tag cloud** is a list of links—usually linked *tags*—displayed in a block and weighted by popularity or some other criteria. The end result is what appears to be a "cloud" of links, like this one, from Flickr.

All time most popular tags

africa amsterdam animals april architecture art asia august australia baby barcelona beach berlin birthday black blackandwhite blue boston bw california cameraphone camping canada canon car cat cats chicago china christmas church city clouds color concert day dc de dog england europe family festival film florida flower flowers food france friends fun garden geotagged germany girl graffiti green halloween hawaii hiking holiday home honeymoon house india ireland island italy japan july june kids la lake landscape light live london losangeles macro may me mexico mountain mountains museum music nature new newyork newyorkcity newzealand night nikon nyc ocean paris park party people photos portrait red river roadtrip rock rome san sanfrancisco scotland sea seattle show sky snow spain spring street summer sun sunset sydney taiwan texas thailand tokyo toronto tour travel tree trees trip uk urban usa vacation vancouver washington water wedding white winter yellow york zoo

Flickr.com was the first major site to offer a tag cloud, but the idea has been copied on countless other sites. So when this designer came to me to review the blog template, I figured, "Cool—let's go with it. Tag clouds are becoming pretty common, so let's see if it works for us, too."

The designer had already done a lot of his decision-making. He started with a simple link list, sorted in order of popularity.

```
user_experience
experience_design
interaction_design
visual_design
articles
books
development
design
code
resources
technology
tools
```

Next, he weighted the list using some programming wizardry to increase the font size of each link based on its relative popularity. To highlight these font size differences, he sorted the list alphabetically.

```
articles
books
code
design
development
experience_design
interaction_design
resources
technology
tools
user_experience
visual_design
```

Then, he removed the line breaks and scrunched the links all together into a "cloud."

articles books code design
development experience_design
interaction_design resources technology
tools user_experience
visual_design

Finally, since the system was capable of displaying both the cloud version and a plain ol' list, he added a Cloud button and a List button to the bottom of the interface for toggling between these two views.

articles books code design
development experience_design
interaction_design resources technology
tools user_experience
visual_design

[Cloud] [List]

It seemed like a good idea at the time.

▶ Justifying Innovation

The innovation in the design was the decision to offer two views. This was the only piece added to the tag-cloud idea that hadn't previously been done in implementations on other sites. And the designer went along with this idea based on a comment from the developer tasked with building the blog template.

"The developer told me the user might want to switch views," he said.

And while thinking I was being rather crafty, I decided to *elevate* instead of innovate. Instead of coming up with this new contribution to tag clouds, why not just leave it alone? We were already improving upon link lists by showing tag clouds in the first place, right? This was enough of an elevation. Adding the buttons was going too far.

I figured that people who understood the logic would benefit from the cloud view, and those who didn't understand it would still see a list of links. No harm, no foul.

I didn't believe that users would spend enough time on the page, staring at that sidebar, to bother wanting to customize it in any way. It wasn't a critical feature that simply *had* to work the way a user wanted it to work—it was a simple list of links. So I told the designer to remove the buttons and show only the cloud.

My argument, I believe, was right. But I also believe I didn't think it through far enough.

When to just say no

Tag clouds are a funny little deviation from the idea of ambient signifiers (discussed in the previous chapter). Technically, they do the same type of thing as my sorted link list example—they employ visual differences to communicate something more than what a flat list can communicate on its own—but tag clouds require something that the sorted link list doesn't.

Knowledge.

To truly benefit from the logic of a tag cloud, you need to know why some links are larger than others and/or why some are darker than others. And therein lies the rub.

Most of the users I watch interact with tag clouds have no idea why some links are larger than others. Extremely few of them even bother to *guess* why some links are larger than others, and of those few people, even fewer of them actually *care.* And clicking the tag links doesn't often result in increased understanding. (These are informal observations, by the way, so feel free to prove me wrong. Just be sure to tell me about it if you do!)

This fact, in and of itself, should mean you can still get away with showing a tag cloud. After all, users don't actually *need* to understand the logic. They still get a list of links, right?

Technically, yes. But tag links are typically very short, containing one or two words at most, and do very little to communicate their purpose.

The combined effect of all these factors is that few people are even *remotely* confident in their understanding of tag clouds.

When I told this designer I didn't believe users would spend enough time on the page to care about customizing the display method for the group of links, I was half right. I was also half wrong.

Sure, he could have added a clear heading to the section of tags—something like "Popular Subjects." He also could have added some instructive text explaining that larger links indicated more popular subjects and smaller links indicated less popular subjects.

In this particular case, however, I should have told him to scrap the tag cloud completely, and just show a short list of subjects, sorted in order of popularity. Why?

Because there was no reason in the world—on *this* page, in *this* scenario, in *this* blog template—to force users to *think*.

There was no reason to ask users to learn why some links were larger than others. Users had no compelling reason to invest energy into learning what the tag cloud meant or why it mattered.

On Flickr, users are often invested in creating large repositories of images to share with their family and friends. On LibraryThing, a book cataloging site, users are invested in, well, cataloging their books. In such cases, the learning curve associated with a tag cloud can be justified. Tag clouds offer a glimpse into how people are using the site, and give them a way to evaluate a lot of information quickly. But on a blog, most people stick around just long enough to read a post, and then they're outta there. As such, a blog template is a terrible place to force users to learn new interaction patterns.

As I said, I didn't believe users would stick around long enough to want to customize the display of the links. What never occurred to me is that it was extremely unlikely users would stick around long enough to learn the function of a tag cloud in the first place. At best, it would make them think when there was no reason to. At worst, users could actually become confused by it.

This is what I *should* have told the designer.

I guess I'm telling him now.

If you're not part of the solution . . .

In the past few chapters, we've looked at layout, branding, navigation, and even how to create ambient signifiers to aid in a user's orientation process.

But part of creating a good first impression is knowing what *not* to show. The tag cloud that went into that blog template way back when was a momentary lapse of reason on my part that could still be affecting users to this day. And though it kills me to know it's out there, I realize that we can't know *every-thing*. Design is a never-ending learning process—there will always be more to know—and some experiments will go wrong no matter how knowledgeable we are.

The important thing is that we continually question the way things are done to make sure we get as close to achieving our intended first impression as possible.

Design should never be left to fate. The way a site looks, how it's laid out, the navigational structure, the elements used to communicate its personality—every last one of these things, down to the way colors and fonts are used, is critical to the first impression (and all those that follow). They all need to be designed intentionally so that the right message is communicated and our users can trust our sites and applications.

And as you'll see in the next three chapters, the buck definitely doesn't stop there. Something as simple as text can have a major impact on how users perceive us, how much they understand about our applications, and how much they care to stick around and keep using our products.

I can't stress this enough. Leave nothing to chance.

Everything is important.

PART II

Learning

Ever seen a big block of text at the top of a page and completely ignored it? Ever seen a confirmation dialog box that asked if you were sure you wanted to cancel an operation, and featured a Cancel button next to an OK button? Ever seen a check-box option for something that lacked any explanation whatsoever?

Most Web users have.

Copy is every bit as important as everything else in an interface. And in most cases, it's all our users have to rely on.

In the moment we're trying to understand what a site is about or how a task is supposed to be completed, the words on a page can mean the difference between building confidence and losing it. They can mean the difference between loving a site and leaving it permanently.

Text can explain the purpose, benefit, and usage of a page, or it can confuse a user to no end, leaving her to guess and potentially make a mistake for which she'll blame herself.

When people use our applications, all they know is what we tell them. Our job, then, is to give them the right information, in as concise and clear a manner as possible. The simple act of changing nouns into *verb-noun pairs* and surfacing the right trigger words (words users seek out that fit into their mental model of how a site works) can have a serious impact on how users perceive our sites. And when words just won't do, other solutions can succeed where text fails.

In the next three stories, we'll look at ways to communicate with our users more clearly. In the first two, we'll look at how text can be modified to create more meaning for users, and in the third story, we'll talk about how to use video when text doesn't quite do the job.

6

Surfacing the Trigger Words

I once worked with a small e-learning company to create a learning management system (LMS) for a major airline, so that its enormous staff of tarmac workers could keep up on security and safety measures and learn new skills to advance their skill sets.

The vast majority of these workers lacked a college education, and this fact seemed to make the human resources folks believe that everything needed to be thoroughly explained to the workers. Although I found this mind-set rather condescending, I saw an opportunity to use it to my advantage when they came to me with a wireframe for the home page of the LMS.

▶ Why Welcome Messages Are Useless

The home-page design contained a big ol' chunk of text that served as a Welcome message. It explained that users could locate courses to take online that would help them learn new things and keep up on safety regulations.

Welcome!

Welcome to the BigJet Course Finder! Here, you can locate courses in various areas of interest. With these courses, you can improve on your current skill set, explore other types of positions in the company, study for certification exams, review safety procedures, and even learn new skills.

To get started, just browse through the course finder interface below, then choose a course and follow the instructions. If you choose a graded course, your score will be submitted to Human Resources as soon as you're done. That's all there is to it!

Course finder

I'm sure you've seen messages like this online at least, oh, a million or so times. But how many of them have you read?

As Jakob Nielsen points out in his Alertbox article, "Blah-Blah Text: Keep, Cut, or Kill?" people don't generally read the text on a Web page—they scan it. Longer introductory text tends to get ignored. That said, shorter blocks of text can attract some attention (providing it's actually *useful*), and as such, can help a user understand what she's looking at.

When we explore a new application, as opposed to an information-heavy site where we focus on reading, we're looking for obvious clues about what the site is for, how it works, and what we need to do to start being productive with it. In other words, we're thinking about *doing*, not *reading*. We want to get things done, so every step we take is about accomplishing something, whatever that something is.

When I saw this Welcome message, for example, I immediately avoided it, focusing on the Course Finder, the primary interactive element on the page.

▶ Designing for Scannability

I did skim through it eventually, however, because it was my job to review the design. But when I went over the block of text, this is what I saw.

Welcome!

Blah blah blah blah blah blah blah blah blah blah blah locate courses blah blah blah blah blah blah blah blah blah blah blah blah blah blah blah blah blah blah blah blah blah blah blah blah blah blah blah blah blah blah blah blah blah blah blah blah blah blah blah blah blah blah blah blah.

Blah blah blah blah blah blah blah blah course finder blah blah blah blah blah blah blah blah blah blah blah blah blah blah blah blah blah blah blah blah blah blah blah blah blah blah blah blah blah blah blah blah blah blah blah blah blah blah blah!

Course finder

This is probably pretty similar to what you see when you read Welcome messages. We're much more interested in getting something done than reading a message that serves absolutely no purpose and doesn't help us accomplish our goals.

The first problem is that the message was titled "Welcome," as though the company was opening the office's front door to receive guests at a holiday party. But this isn't a holiday party, it's the Web. And these aren't guests. They're people with a lot of work to do, interrupting their lives to get through some company-mandated safety course or learn a new skill to try to earn a promotion.

They don't care about being welcomed. They care about finding a course.

So first, let's give them some confidence that they're on the right page by changing the title to "Find a course."

Find a course

Blah blah blah blah blah blah blah blah blah blah blah locate courses blah blah blah blah blah blah blah blah blah blah blah blah blah blah blah blah blah blah blah blah blah blah blah blah blah blah blah blah blah blah blah blah blah blah blah blah blah blah blah blah blah blah blah blah.

Blah blah blah blah blah blah blah blah course finder blah blah blah blah blah blah blah blah blah blah blah blah blah blah blah blah blah blah blah blah blah blah blah blah blah blah blah blah blah blah blah blah blah blah blah blah blah blah!

Course finder

Better. But that silly block of text is still there. Let's make it useful.

Call-to-action phrases

A **call-to-action** phrase is a set of words used to inspire people to take action. It resembles a command, such as "Go to your room," but lacks the hostility.

You've seen them a million times or so as well. They're statements like, "Save changes," "Read more," and "Sign in,"

They have the added benefit of being very scannable. Because they often come in the form of verb-noun pairs, they do a very good job of telling the user exactly what will happen next, and still lets him feel like he's directing the software.

Using "Find a course" as a page heading lets the user know what to do on the page, but the large block of text does little to offer more detail.

The next step, then, was to get rid of the text and replace it with something short and concise that contained a call-to-action statement.

In this case, I didn't even need a short paragraph that explained the central purpose of the page. Sometimes all that's needed is a single line that explains what can be done on the page to simultaneously explain its purpose, benefit, and usage.

Through sheer determination, and about five seconds' worth of time, I managed to overcome major adversity and pare down two full paragraphs of text to a single sentence.

Find a course

Locate a course, then click its title to get started.

Course finder

All right, it wasn't that difficult.

The new version of the page cut straight to the point. No wasting users' time here.

Unfortunately, it wasn't as simple as all that.

The client didn't want to give up the Welcome text. Apparently, someone in the marketing department had worked hard on it and really spent some quality time thinking out how to word it *just right.*

"What if the users need more information?" they asked.

"They won't," I replied.

That argument didn't work too well.

What ended up being the clincher for this human resources team was an argument that went something like this:

"These people only have high school educations. I'd be surprised if they read it at all. [*Chuckle, chuckle.*]"

Although I completely disagreed with their assessment of their own workers' intelligence, empathizing with the client made them think that shortening the text was *their* idea.

They went with my version. And as far as I know, there were never any questions about how to use the page or what could be done there.

The major lesson to be learned?

A single sentence can be far more meaningful to a user than even the best-written paragraph. What matters is not that there's plenty of information, but that the information that's there really matters.

7

Labeling the Interface

Recently, I did a usability review for an e-learning company working on the second version of their featured product, a Web-based course-builder tool.

The product was designed primarily for e-learning developers. The idea was that people who already knew quite a bit about e-learning courseware and score-tracking systems could build their courses in less time by using this tool to create slides based on a selection of templates. Users would create a new course, create the slides they needed, choose templates for each one, and then fill out some forms to create the content for each slide.

The thing that kept popping into my head as I reviewed the application is that it could very easily work for a wider range of audiences. Instead of focusing entirely on people who already knew a lot about how to develop e-learning courses, some relatively simple design tweaks could make the application usable by instructional designers, human-resources teams, and many others.

Naturally, it occurred to me that widening the audience would translate to more money for the company. The client was understandably agreeable to this idea, so I focused my recommendations on ways to accomplish this.

I started on the Create Course screen, where users were to enter a project ID and title, and choose from a variety of options to set up a new course.

New Project

New project ID

Tracking

Choose ...

Course completion

Choose ...

Course Properties

Title

Options

☐ Narration button   ☐ Exit button
☐ Glossary button   ☐ Audio button
☐ Page numbering   ☐ Persistent index
☐ Use index tooltip   ☐ Use course logo

Page transition

Choose ...

Transition time

Transition direction

Choose ...

Because I had no idea what would be acceptable as a project ID, I entered "My Project." After I finished the form, I got this error message.

Error   **X**

The project id "My Project" is invalid.

Um, thanks. But why is it invalid? How do I make it valid? What does a valid project ID look like?

This particular screen assumed a lot of knowledge. And then it put labels on those assumptions.

▶ Stop Labeling Your Assumptions

There are loads of input fields and check boxes and radio buttons on the Web that lack context. They ask users to do things without explaining what those things mean.

We often make assumptions about how much our users will understand about our applications. We assume a user will know what we meant when we wrote "Persistent index" next to a check box, or "New project ID" next to an input field. We assume, and then we label our assumptions.

Right there in the interface, we tell our users that in order to use our software, they have to know things *only we could know.* We tell them they have to read our minds.

Funny that we so often accuse our users of being the faulty part of the equation, isn't it?

Here's how you fix the problem.

Look at each and every label in your application and ask yourself if someone who has never seen the app before will know what it means. Write a list of all the "no" answers and either change those labels so they're more meaningful or add instructive elements that explain them (text, screenshot, short video, and so on).

Also keep a list of "yes" answers. When you're done writing, show all your yes's to three people who have never touched your app before.

When you're done, I suspect you'll need to change a few more labels.

Don't feel bad, though. I changed at least three of my own earlier today.

For this usability review, I recommended starting with a simple solution to the project ID issue. I just added a bit of text that showed what an acceptable project ID looked like.

New Project

New project ID
No spaces (e.g. "MyProjectID")

Tracking
Choose ...

Course completion
Choose ...

Course Properties

Title

Options
- Narration button
- Glossary button
- Page numbering
- Use index tooltip
- Exit button
- Audio button
- Persistent index
- Use course logo

Page transition
Choose ...

Transition time

Transition direction
Choose ...

From there, it was as simple as extending the idea to the rest of the controls on the screen.

First, I added links to Help articles next to most of the controls. Next, I added instructive text to input fields to help explain what was acceptable as an entry. Finally, I changed a few of the labels to make them more explicit. For example, "Transition time" became "Transition time, in seconds."

New Project

New project ID
No spaces (e.g. "MyProjectID")

Tracking method (What's this?)
Choose ...

Course completion (What's this?)
Choose ...

Course Properties

Title
This will appear in the published course.

Options
- Narration button (?)   - Exit button (?)
- Glossary button (?)   - Audio button (?)
- Page numbering (?)   - Persistent index (?)
- Use index tooltip (?)   - Use course logo (?)

Page transition (?)
Choose ...

Transition time, in seconds (What's this?)
e.g. 1.5

Transition direction (What's this?)
Choose ...

Instead of labeling our assumptions, we need to assume the users know absolutely nothing about our software and subsequently give them the information that will help them understand.

Instructive text, **What's This?** links, and clear labels usually do the trick.

8

Beyond Words and Onto Video

Half my job is about pointing out the obvious, but once in a while, something hits me that is so obvious, apparently even *I* can't see it.

One of these lightning bolts came while I was working on a usability review for a client.

I found myself trying very hard to explain, with the written word, that an input field in a form wasn't doing a good job of explaining to users that it had a character limit. Only 50 characters could be entered into the field, but nothing explained this fact, and when I reached the character limit, new characters simply stopped appearing. It looked like my keyboard had broken. Suddenly, I could no longer type.

For whatever reason, that day I was having a particularly difficult time getting the wording just right so that my explanation made sense. I thought about taking a screenshot or two, but how was that going to help? All the client would see in the screenshot was an input field with a bunch of characters in it. It wouldn't explain the sinking, remarkably inaccurate feeling that my keyboard had broken.

I thought about writing out the steps needed to repeat the issue. Somehow, though, this seemed like a lot of work. If I couldn't word a simple explanation to my own satisfaction, I couldn't expect the words in a sequence of steps to come out any better.

And that's when the lightning bolt hit.

Video, you idiot. Video!

▶ A Moving Picture Is Worth 10,000 Words

Instructive video clips, known as **screencasts**, are used on all kinds of sites these days, likely because it has become so incredibly easy to create video for the Web.

Basecamp (by 37signals), for example, includes a screencast on each one of its "blank slates" (pages devoid of user-created content).

This a great use for a screencast, and it's the perfect place to show one. The user can quickly learn how to do something in the application at the exact moment he needs to know about it. I very often use Basecamp to manage client projects, and it's quite comforting to know these videos will show up for my clients, most of whom are using Basecamp for the first time and need to get up to speed.

And going far above and beyond the call of duty are the videos created for "The Common Craft Show." These movies are not screencasts, per se, because they're not recordings of a computer screen, but rather are lively, engaging digital stories about new or frequently misunderstood technologies.

The video shown here discusses energy-saving, compact fluorescent light bulbs. Common Craft has also created videos about wikis, RSS, and even online photo sharing.

The videos are the result of a painstaking process of creating a series of drawings on posterboard and filming a narrative by stepping through each drawing, complete with the comic assistance of the narrator's hands, to tell a story about how the technology works and benefits people.

Using video to communicate problems

Having suddenly remembered all the wonderful ways to use video for communication, I realized I could use video to explain the problem with the input field to my client instead of, well, *explaining it*. Pretty obvious, right?

So I quickly recorded a video of my screen as I tried to enter more than 50 characters into the input field. I recorded the audio track as well so the client could hear me banging away at my keyboard to no avail.

I even narrated a little to articulate what a user might think in this exact situation.

"My keyboard . . . has broken. It's just stopped working. I have no idea why. Maybe it came unplugged. Nope. That's not it. Maybe I'm a moron. Nope. I have an MBA. Maybe I need to restart my computer. Too bad—I was just starting to like this site. Oh well."

A whopping 20 seconds later, I was done. I played it back to make sure it recorded properly. Less than a minute after having the revelation, I had a solution that was more effective than any I had thought up previously.

When I gave the video to the client, along with the rest of the usability review, they understood it. It's hard to argue with video.

Using video to communicate ideas

Immediately after this little success, I realized that if I could use video to illustrate *problems,* I could also use it to illustrate *ideas.* You know, in the same way a prototype illustrates ideas. It puts something in front of the client that they can *watch.* And think about. And watch again. No interpretation needed.

I could record a video that explains how an interaction is supposed to occur and narrate it rather than writing it all out. You know, like the video version of a prototype. Like a prototype version of a screencast. And with that, a word popped into my head.

Protocast.

Genius. Genius, I tell you! If you hear a little *"Bwa-hahahaha!"* in your head, that's the echo of me cackling like a crazy man over my own brilliance.

OK, so I was overcompensating for being such an idiot earlier.

Regardless, I immediately found every excuse in the world to include protocasts in the set of design documents I handed over to clients. These simple recordings save me huge amounts of time and often communicate far more than the step-by-step use cases that I typically include with my designs.

▶ The Ridiculously Simple Art of Protocasting

Creating a protocast—or **screencast**, for instructive purposes on a site—is a fairly quick and painless process if you have the tools for it and spend a couple of minutes to prepare.

First, figure out what needs to be communicated. In most cases, I simply need to show how an interaction should work, so all I need to do is show a series of screen states and explain what the user can do in each one to arrive at the next screen state and complete the interaction.

For example, when doing a protocast for a five-star–rating interface, you need to show the default state, what to click to set a rating, what happens on the screen when this click occurs, what to do to complete the rating, and how the screen looks when it's completed. Pretty straightforward, but this means you need a way to create a simple prototype so you can click through each state.

I prefer to use OmniGraffle, because I use it a lot and am comfortable with it, but you can use Adobe Flash, Microsoft Visio (Windows only), Gliffy (a Flash-based Web application similar to Visio), or even Microsoft PowerPoint.

With Flash, for example, you can create a series of frames, each frame showing a different screen state (using wireframes or higher-resolution composites), and simply create button actions for each clickable item. Then publish the file and use a screen-recording tool to record the steps you take to complete the interaction.

There are a variety of tools available to record actions onscreen. I use Snapz Pro X (Mac only), which makes it just as simple to record a movie as it is to create a screenshot. A Windows alternative is Camtasia Studio, made by Tech-Smith, which works in a similar fashion.

The newest, and arguably the coolest screen-recording and screenshot tool is a new product by TechSmith called Jing, available for free.

Once installed, Jing can be used to create screenshots or movies with just a couple of clicks, and anything created with Jing can be shared via a URL that is automatically created for you or via your Screencast.com account.

In other words, when you're done recording a movie, you can click the Share icon to upload the movie to Screencast.com. You can either paste the URL (which is automatically copied to the Clipboard once the video is uploaded), or you can save the movie and retrieve it later.

When words just won't do, consider using video to help your users—and your clients—get up to speed.

Oh, and if you happened to have thought up the concept of protocasts before I did, please don't tell me about it. I'd like to continue believing it was my idea.

Thank you.

PART III

Searching

Changing from a passive site visitor to an active user is as simple as shifting the goal from browsing to searching. And searching, as we all know, is one of the most basic and important tasks we can perform online. Google has taught us that everything we can possibly imagine can be found in seconds by a good search engine.

Of course, not all search engines can be as good as Google. In fact, many of them do a horrible job of providing access to information. This is not necessarily because the algorithms used to run searches are terrible—sometimes they're quite good.

The problem, more often than not, is the interface.

The fact is, most people who have used search engines have used Google, and most people who have used Google have accepted it as the gold standard of search perfection. If it's not Google, it's crap.

So how can we compete? How can we get users on our sites the information they want without making them resort to leaving the site and using Google? How can we help our users find the right information quickly, at the exact moment they need it? How can we help them understand the search function and the results in the moment they encounter them?

To answer this question, I offer three stories about different facets of search. The first is about search, the second about finding our way through the results, and the third about refining search criteria to get more effective results.

All these stories, of course, are about creating positive moments that will keep users on your site instead of someone else's.

9

Making Suggestions

Shortly before DoTheRightThing.com (DTRT) launched in 2006, DTRT founders Rod Ebrahimi and Ryan Mickle approached me about doing a usability review on their designs. And I must have been feeling awfully generous in that moment, because upon hearing about their idea, I offered them my review free of charge. Simply put, I really believed in the idea and I wanted to help out.

Rod and Ryan were out to change a little piece of the world. They had created a home for user-generated content focused entirely around the behavior of corporations. When a company like Adobe or Yahoo does something the community thinks is karmically good, site members can post a story about the deed in an effort to bring attention to it and encourage other companies to step up and "do the right thing." Likewise, when a company does something less than savory, these posts can serve to encourage the community at large to speak out against the company. Members can also rate the social impact of each story as they see fit.

It's a noble idea, and I'm proud to be associated with DTRT.

Before they could change the world, however, they desperately needed to change the single most important task flow on the site: the process of posting a new story.

After three days of wondering how to post a new story as I did my review, I never figured it out. I had to ask.

It turns out that in the original design, you had to click a Companies tab and choose a company name before you could post a story about a company's good (or bad) deed.

Aside from being inefficient, the design made it terribly difficult to figure out *how* to post a new story. After all, you had to be on a company's detail page to do it, and there was no reason to go to a company's page when you were thinking about posting a story. For the posting process to be obvious, there needed to be a way to start the process from anywhere on the site.

I suggested they stick the Submit New Story button on every page of the site, and then have users either choose from a list of companies to write about or enter a new one and post the story on the next page.

DTRT liked this idea, and I'm happy to say that when they showed me their solution a couple of weeks later, they surprised me by building something much better than what I had anticipated.

Instead of simply dumping a list of company-name links on a page and asking users to click one, they opted for a search function. More specifically, an *auto-complete* search function.

▶ Using Auto-complete as a Poka-yoke Device

Poka-yoke is Japanese for **error-proofing**, and poka-yoke devices can be created that either detect an error or prevent it from occurring.

The **auto-complete** design pattern is an example of a poka-yoke prevention device.

Auto-complete is the fancy name given to those fancy input fields that attempt to *guess* what is being entered into the field and dynamically complete it. Some versions show the most likely completed term right there in the search box, while others display a list of possible matches from which the user can choose.

In either case, auto-complete can help users prevent typographical errors and ensure their searches are more effective.

In DTRT's case, it also attempts to prevent users from entering a variation of a company name that already exists in the database when posting a new story.

Step 1: Search for a company to write about:

```
Ad
Adobe Systems (Macromedia, Photoshop, Flash)
Innocent Drinks
Tesla Motors
HMRC
Sterling National Bank
Sterling National Bank
Sterling National Bank
ePrep
Accenture
Make Money on Google Adsense
```

For example, when attempting to write a story about Adobe Systems, typing the letters *Ad* produces a list of company names that begin with those letters. Adobe happens to be the first one, so a user can simply choose *Adobe Systems* from the list and move on to the next step. If *Adobe* hadn't appeared, the user would likely have entered whatever she *thought* was the full name of the company (likely *Adobe*), and DTRT would end up with multiple database entries for the same company.

This would result in multiple pages about the same company, none of which would contain a complete listing of the stories posted about it.

Auto-complete also helps prevent mistakes in the user's search. Instead of potentially misspelling a company name and finding no results, DTRT users usually see the correct company name appear in the list of suggestions after entering just a few characters.

Auto-complete even eliminates the need for paginated search results. Because the results appear immediately—within the page—there is no need to wait for search results to load on a new page.

Most of all, though, many users simply appreciate auto-complete, saying "it just works" and indicating that it makes them trust a site more because the developers made the extra effort to make things really easy to use.

The auto-complete solution has some remarkable benefits, but it also has a few caveats.

The pitfalls

In *Designing the Obvious,* I pointed out that Google Suggest offered a solution that blurred the line between detection and prevention devices.

Well, it turns out that auto-complete isn't nearly as helpful for users performing broad searches on sites such as Google Suggest and Yahoo Instant Search as it is for users running searches against a limited set of data, like a catalog of bicycle parts.

Google Suggest, in other words, does a better job of illustrating the caveats of auto-complete than it does teaching us how to error-proof a design.

First, users who stare at their keyboards often fail to notice the suggestions, rendering them all but useless. Some do eventually look up from their keyboards and notice the suggestions accidentally, but many simply hit Enter before looking up and never notice the suggestions at all.

Second, users often choose a suggested search term over their own, even when their own would have been more effective.

For example, a user searching for information about designing intranet portals would likely search for, well, "designing intranet portals." But many users who start entering this term will notice the suggested search terms and choose "designing intranets" instead.

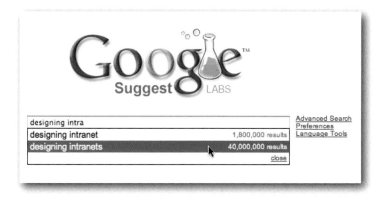

This *appears* to happen because users either think the suggested terms are going to yield more effective results than their own search terms, or that the search terms are what the search-engine developers *want* them to search.

The latter of these two reasons is ridiculous—I know—but many people think this way. They think that if they're being told—or at least guided—to do something, it's because the site telling them to do it is smarter than they are, and therefore they should listen.

In any case, auto-completing search terms in the context of a broad search can inadvertently compel users to use less effective search terms than they would have used on their own had they ignored the suggestions.

Third, you have to be careful not to jump the gun with your suggestions.

In Yahoo Instant Search, typing *des* yields current financial data for Wisdom Tree. Doing the same thing in Google Suggest reveals "desperate housewives" as the most likely choice. But clearly, the entry of three characters from the word *design* isn't nearly enough for Yahoo or Google to know what information the user is seeking.

Avoid showing suggestions until enough characters have been typed for the suggestion to be meaningful. Since there is no magic number for how quickly a suggested search term should be displayed, consider using three or four as the cutoff. As in, avoid showing suggestions until the user has entered enough letters to run a meaningful search.

Finally, as with just about anything created through Ajax and DHTML, accessibility is a concern when using auto-complete.

Screen readers read loaded pages in order from top to bottom. As such, anything that magically appears on a page *after* it has been loaded needs to notify the screen reader of the change and give it immediate access to the changed portion of the page so it can be "read" by the user.

The right solution at the right time

Despite these caveats, we can help many of our users acquire information more quickly with auto-complete, prevent them from making search mistakes, prevent multiple database entries for the same data, and offer up a little something extra for users to appreciate in the moment they seek out information on our sites.

For DoTheRightThing, auto-complete was the perfect solution. Instead of creating a cumbersome story-posting process, they *did the right thing* by speeding up the process and making it more effective.

10

Getting Through the Results

When we run a search on the Web, the step right after entering a search term and clicking a Search button is usually finding our way through a sea of results to locate the information we need. This simple act has become extremely commonplace, especially since so many Web experiences now begin on Google.com.

We head to Google, search, find a relevant link, and click it. When we need something else, we head back to Google.

As such, the Google interface has become second nature to many people. Even novice Web users point their browsers straight to the legendary minimal design almost religiously as a first step toward learning new things, shopping, or even finding a site for which we already know the domain. (Yes, many people—perhaps even you—type a URL into Google's search box and click on the first result to access the domain.)

This fact caused me some trouble while working on a forum application. I realized that even something as simple as a pagination interface for a search-results page could become a pain point for users if designed poorly. After spending a couple of weeks working with the development for this forum application, I was shown the implementation of the search-results pages.

And the pagination interface was, well, not so good.

First, the link for the current page—page 1—was clickable, but didn't need to be. After all, the user is already on the page, right?

Second, there was no indication in the design which page was current. Nothing was done to make the current page number stand out—it looked identical to all the other page links.

Also, the left-pointing arrow on page 1 didn't make sense because there's nothing to go back to on the first page of search results. The right arrow could be clicked, but the left one could not.

The label for the interface, Page, was nonessential. It wasn't necessarily doing any harm, but it was a little awkward since there was no indication of the current page.

The numbered links were quite small. They were displayed using a font size typical of body text, but since each link contained only one character, it was difficult to roll over them with the mouse to click.

Finally, the interface was placed in the top-right corner of the list of search results. This broke the convention set by all of the major search sites, including Google, MSN, Yahoo, and others.

Now, I often advocate trying to challenge standards, but it's vitally important to remember that if you're going to challenge standards, the goal is to *improve them*. If you're not improving the standard, your users will gain nothing from the new design, and they could potentially lose the benefits of recognizing the design from other sites and immediately understanding how to use it.

▶ Trusting the Standards That Actually Work Well

Every so often, something becomes *so* standard that deviating from it is simply bad form. Probably thanks to Google, pagination interfaces fall into this category.

Google's pagination interface is immensely recognizable—not just because of its use on Google, but because it has been copied on countless other sites, including other major search sites.

Everywhere you look, there are pagination interfaces that vary only slightly from one to the next. Each one has a **Previous** link, a **Next** link, and a set of numbered links in between. And most of them do something to make the current page number stand out from the other links.

With this in mind, I started making changes to the pagination interface in this forum application.

First, I removed the Page label, created a *disabled* state for the left arrow, and moved the arrows to either side of the collection of numbered links. I did this so that the first thing in the interface was the option to go back a page. For the sake of consistency, I also changed the arrow color to match the links.

Next, I increased the font size a bit and changed the style of the number for the current page to make it stand out from the numbered links. To do this, I made it plain text instead of a link, changed its color to red, and increased its font size. I also increased the size of the arrows, to generally make each element in the interface easier to click.

Finally, I added links for **Previous** and **Next**, placing them next to their corresponding arrows. Technically, there is no need for these words in most cases—the arrows would probably do the trick on their own—but the large text makes the hit area for each of the most prevalent links larger and easier to hit. Making the interface a tiny bit easier to use makes the moment of interaction a tiny bit better.

Oh, and of course I moved it from the top-right of the results listings to bottom-center, so that it would be spotted more readily by all those jillions of Web users who expect it to be there.

By relying on the standards in this case, the difficulty of using—or even *finding*—the pagination interface was decreased. Google and the like have made pagination a very common design pattern, and they've all implemented these interfaces in very similar ways. And this very standard solution is actually quite usable even for beginning users. As such, it's simply better to rely on the standards than do anything that deviates from it at risk of breaking a user's expectations.

Offering a way back to the results

Before we move on, there is one other thing I'd like to note about search-results pages.

Occasionally, I see a design for a landing page that is accessed from search results that offers no way to *return* to the results.

When this happens, the user either relies on the almighty Back button or runs a new search from the landing page. But I'm of the camp that believes a user should never have to rely on the Back button. The site navigation should always offer a way for users to get to and fro without relying on browser tools.

Because of this, I often stick a little something into my own designs that serves this purpose explicitly. It looks very much like what Gmail offers.

When a Gmail user accesses mail tagged with a specific label (all messages can be assigned a label, similar to a folder, that appears in the sidebar navigation), and then reads one of the messages under that label, Gmail offers up a **Back to** link.

In the image above, the link lets me go "Back to Newsletters." Newsletters, as you may guess, is a label I created for any incoming mail from newsletter subscriptions. Without the **Back to** link, the only way to return to the messages with the Newsletters label would be to find the word *Newsletters* in the sidebar again and click it.

At best, this would be inefficient. At worst, I wouldn't realize that this was the solution and I'd click something else by accident and completely lose my place.

When designing results pages, consider adding something like this to any page that's accessed from a results page (for example, Home > Search results > Product page).

My designs (in wireframe form) typically look something like this.

This simple **Back to Search Result**s link, highlighted by a colored background, offers users a way out. It gives them an anchor they can rely on without resorting to browser tools.

Sites should be able to pass what I call "The Browserless Self-Test," which involves hiding the toolbar, Favorites bar, and so on in a browser and navigating a site without any aid from browser tools whatsoever. If your site passes the test, you can call it a day and go eat a sandwich.

Back to links and pagination interfaces are very basic ideas, but if they're done poorly, they can become a point of frustration for users. When something is as common as these ideas, it's best to rely on the standards and help your users get through your site without having to learn anything new.

11

Refining Your Search

Most people rely strictly on that simple and recognizable input field located on most sites, accompanied by a Search button. And when they truly need more control over their searches, there is often an Advanced Search option of some kind to turn to.

But how advanced does it need to get? More specifically, how complicated do the Advanced options need to be for a user to find what she needs?

In many cases, Advanced Search is a screen chock-full of options that can quickly become overwhelming. Take Google's Advanced Search page, for example.

In many cases, this level of granularity is simply unnecessary. Although more experienced users or users with very specific needs may venture through advanced options on occasion, these options can usually be presented via a simpler interface than is often given.

This was the case on a recent project where I was tasked with the redesign of a product catalog for a digital download company. Quick Search, as they called it, was simple enough—just an input field and a Search button—but Advanced Search was a whole different animal. Whenever a user clicked the <u>Advanced Search</u> link, he was presented with this screen.

Search content				
Search in:	Text ⬍	for:	"interface design"	☒
and in:	Subject ⬍	for:	"web design"	☒
and in:	Publication years ⬍	for:	From: 2006 To: 2008	☒
and in:	License type ⬍	for:	All license types ⬍	☒
and in:	Document type ⬍	for:	All document types ⬍	☒
and in:	Title ⬍	for:	"interface"	☒

(Search)   (Start over)

This Advanced Search page wasn't nearly as complicated as Google's, but there were still several things about it that could be substantially improved.

For starters, all of the options were shown at once, presumably so the user could see them all and simply edit whichever ones she needed. But this approach often makes one of those pesky cartoon thought bubbles appear over a user's head:

"Do I need to fill this whole thing out? What happens if I only fill out part of it?"

Upon closer inspection, she may notice that the little X icons can be used to delete rows of criteria from the form, triggering another thought bubble:

"Does this mean each unneeded row *must* be removed for the form to work correctly? And if I delete one too many rows, or change my mind and want to add one at some point, how do I do that? Do I have to hit Start Over and do the whole thing from scratch?"

And, of course:

"If I save this search, how do I access it again later on?"

Clearing up all these questions was a simple matter of cleaning up the form.

▶ Keeping Advanced Simple

First, I decided to keep the default Quick Search option, because it was perfectly appropriate, useful, and usable. This is where most people would start their searches, and it was done in a very standard way, so I saw no reason so change it.

To speed things up in the new design, and to make the form more effective and understandable, I wanted to avoid sending users to a new page to fill out a complicated form.

To start, I used the **inline expand** pattern, where new elements are essentially dropped into a page, pushing other content downward.

This way, clicking the <u>Advanced</u> link would cause the new form to magically appear without requiring the user to wait for a new page to load.

Simple enough. But the real problem wasn't so much the page-load time as it was that ugly form.

Progressive disclosure in action

Now, most people would never bother editing each and every row in the form. And of the few that would, even fewer would do it every single time. Usually, the people that do need advanced search options only need a *few* options.

In other words, human behavior tells us that we don't need all the rows to show up at once. What we really need is a simple solution that will work *in most cases,* and a way to increase the number of options should it become necessary.

Progressive disclosure is the perfect solution in times like these.

Simply put, **progressive disclosure** is a design method that entails progressively revealing more and more options as they are needed—based on user input—instead of showing them all by default.

Dialog boxes are often created this way. For example, an <u>Advanced Options</u> link could reveal more options within the dialog box. These options are hidden by default, and appear only when the user explicitly clicks a link to make them appear.

To apply the idea to the Advanced Search form, I replaced the six rows of criteria with a single row and an option to add more.

This way, a user could simply add one row at a time as needed, but she would never be overwhelmed by a suddenly appearing boatload of options.

I also got rid of the Start Over button. Why? Because, well, when was the last time you actually witnessed someone click this type of option? Far more often than not, users don't want to start from scratch; they want to modify something in particular and that's it. So away it went.

(Incidentally, this is also true of other types of Web forms. The Clear Form options we often see are remarkably unnecessary.)

Encouraging interaction

The one row I left showing was the one already accounted for by the Quick Search. In this case, the option was to search in Text for *aviation*. But obviously, a user who has clicked to see Advanced search options will want to refine his search beyond what he's already done. To remedy this, I added a second row and left it empty.

This approach provided users a way to see how to add criteria to the search, and in theory, it would compel them to start adding options.

The only problem left was that the Quick Search was still active, and the appearance of two distinct Search buttons could cause some confusion.

The simple solution was to disable Quick Search (the top Search button).

While I was at it, I changed the **Advanced** link to **Hide advanced** options, so that the user would have a way to cancel the interaction and go back to Quick Search.

Progressive disclosure is a simple concept, and it can be applied to most Web applications in one way or another. Here, we used it to simplify an advanced search form, but elsewhere it can be used to tuck away expert-level features or even provide access to less common configuration options.

And if you have a boss with a lot of bad ideas that absolutely must be built out, you can use progressive disclosure to hide most of them.

Just don't tell him I said it was OK.

PART IV

Diving In

Assuming we've gotten our proverbial user sufficiently oriented to the site, it's time to help him dive in—to learn more, sign up, and start using the application.

Each one of these interaction touch points is an opportunity to create a fluid, pleasant moment.

We can offer screencasts or other marketing-friendly video clips to help users learn more about a service or application fairly easily (as described in Chapter 8, "Beyond Words and Onto Video"), but the design of the interaction itself needs to leave users feeling—again—productive, respected, and smart. And since there's no de facto standard for video playback on the Web, the first story in this part is about designing a video player that works well in myriad situations.

And once we've convinced a user to sign up, she'll be faced with a registration process, and Web forms are *filled* with potential errors. Even the simplest form can lead to confusion. Most forms are simply thrown up on the screen without much thought, using default HTML controls. They're built exactly the same way millions of other forms are built—without feedback mechanisms, inline validation, or designs that support a user's mental model.

In fact, although I always start out the design of a new form by thinking how mundane it is to create yet another one, I often end up really enjoying it, because even simple registration forms have requirements and constraints and challenges. Each one comes out a little different than all the others.

I've watched a lot of people use a lot of forms, and I've learned what can make them boring and tedious, and conversely, what can make them a painless, almost enjoyable step in using an application.

Because of this, I offer you several stories about the design of Web forms, ranging from the very simple to the wickedly complex. These stories focus on form layout, inline validation, *chunking* longer forms into meaningful steps, labeling, retrieving passwords, and even handling conditions within forms.

With any luck, you'll start seeing forms in a whole new way and realize the incredible impact they can have on a user's experience.

First, though, a look at how video playback controls can be improved to help users deal with video on the Web.

12

Standardizing Playback Controls

Handling video playback on the Web is a pretty basic idea. You create an interface for controlling the video and then simply stream the video into the player. But for some reason, video players online vary as wildly as, well, anything else.

YouTube, Yahoo, CNN, NYTimes, and other sites have all come up with decent players that could easily become a standard, but developers don't seem to be learning from the majors and leveraging these designs on their own sites. Still, some of the major sites seem to be learning from *each other*, incrementally approaching a more standardized method of handling playback controls. And that's what we'll explore here. We'll take a look at how some of the most used players on the Web are designed in an effort to create a composite of a player that works well in most situations.

Now, I've never actually needed to design a video player for a client, despite the fact that I was an Adobe Flash developer in a past life, so I designed one for fun. Something I believe will work well for a variety of sites and applications.

Through this, I hope to show you how simple it is to learn from and improve upon something that has already been done a million times.

▶ The Mystery of Programming the VCR

To improve upon video players, you must first understand the ins and outs of existing player designs, so let's take a look at a few of the most popular players.

First, the NYTimes.com player.

This is a fairly typical video player in that it displays the length of the video, the current elapsed time, a volume control, a Play/Pause button, and a progress bar. But the fact that it's typical doesn't mean it's problem-free.

First, the scrub handle (the handle you drag to reach different points on the video time line) looks ridiculously difficult to use. It's narrow and tiny. The hit area for the handle is actually a relatively good size for the graphic, but it looks very small. This, I believe, sets an expectation in a user's mind that it will be difficult to use.

Second, the slider for the volume control is quite small. Older users, particularly those with arthritis or other mobility issues in their hands, may have trouble moving the control with much precision.

CNN.com's video player has similar issues.

The volume slider is very small and can be difficult to manipulate. The text is also very small, which can make it difficult to read for any user with even slight vision problems.

That said, there are a couple of things I really like about the **CNN.com** player.

First, CNN resisted the urge to auto-play the featured video. This means less bandwidth is used up on the initial load of the page, and it means users who don't want to watch the featured video aren't forced to stop it manually so they can peruse the page in peace.

Second, when the page first loads, the player offers a large play button in the center of the video pane. This is a major tip-off to users that the image shown is from the video and is not a static image (the other major tip-off is the visible set of playback controls). It's also an easy, obvious way to start the video should the user choose to watch it. Two good things rolled up into a single button.

The YouTube player offers a large play button as well. (The player shown here is the version we often see embedded into pages on sites other than YouTube.)

The YouTube player has several problems, however.

First, although clicking the Play button plays the video within the page, clicking anywhere else on the stopped video launches YouTube in a new window. This breaks the user's expectation that the video will simply start playing.

Second, the time display shows only the remaining time, not the total time for the video.

Users accustomed to seeing the current and total time on YouTube itself are shown something different on other sites, but there is no good reason for this difference.

And, of course, the text shown and the controls are all quite small.

Finally, the title of the video isn't part of the embedded player. So when someone wants to show a YouTube video on their own site or blog, they have to state somewhere in the text what video is shown. This often means toggling back and forth between browser windows to determine the name and write it down.

Isn't the key to YouTube's success the ability to embed videos on your own site so you can share them with your own audience? Why would they exclude the title of the video when showing it would make this process so much easier for YouTube users?

In sum, there are quite a few things that each of these players does right, and several things each does poorly. The idea here is to learn from what they do well.

But wait—there's something better

Before I go on, though, I want to point out another player that I'm quite fond of that doesn't come from one of the most popular sites on the planet. It's the video player for **TED.com**, home of video versions of the legendary TED talks.

Filmed Feb 2006; Posted Jun 2006

02:05 | 16:23   Ratings

Here, Al Gore tells us what we can do to help solve the climate crisis.

The controls are a decent size; the text is in a more standard font size and is therefore more readable; and the top-left corner offers some additional information about the video, such as when it was filmed and posted.

(TED doesn't need to include the title for the video in the player itself because TED videos can't be embedded into other sites unless you find a version of one on YouTube. Ironic, isn't it?)

Because the video is over 16 minutes long, it's been lovingly divided into several chapters, and users have been given a way to jump to each one via a menu system in the player.

Nice, huh? All you need to do is roll over the video pane and this menu system magically appears.

My only real issue with the TED player is that it offers no indication that rolling over the video pane produces the menu system for navigating to chapters within the video. The only way to discover this is by accident, while moving your mouse around the screen, probably for some other reason.

The only other issue I see is that clock graphic is incredibly small and is at risk of being totally useless to anyone with worse than 20/20 vision. And without the clock graphic, one can only assume the numbers are related to time. Without an explicit label, one must think about what the numbers mean. And we pesky human beings seem to prefer to avoid thinking in general.

Learning from the best and improving the rest

That said, the TED.com player is arguably one of the best on the Web. As such, it makes a great starting point for the design of a new, general-purpose player that works well in most cases.

To turn it into something a little more universally useful and effective, I wanted to address each of the things I thought were wrong with it, and then swap out the ratings button to provide access to the menu system for chapters.

In short, I wanted to do this.

In this version, I added the title of the video at the top-left corner, replaced the tiny clock graphic with a Time label, and changed the Ratings button into a Chapters button.

Clicking the Chapters button now opens the menu system for accessing each chapter in the video.

But before you start thinking about all that extra work you'll have to do to create chapter divisions in all your videos, I should point out that yes, I do realize not every video has or needs chapter divisions.

So I set up one more rule for the player: if there are no chapters, scrap the Chapters button.

Now, the player offers all the core functionality it needs to offer, presents relatively easy-to-use controls, legible text, relevant information about the video (length, elapsed time, the title, and the dates it was filmed and posted).

To finish it off, I decided to leave it in a stopped state by default when the page loads, to avoid that annoying auto-play problem; and to stick a nice, large play button in the center of the video pane whenever the video is stopped.

Voilà!

Hey—if you ever need a design for a video player for your site, give me a ring. I've got a good one for you.

Oh, wait.

13

Nailing Form Layout

Fortunately, the vast majority of forms we encounter on a daily basis online are decently short. They consist of only a few fields, maybe a drop-down list or two, and a button. And they exist to help us get to things we want, enabling us to register for a new site or application, make a purchase, or contact a company.

But have you ever wondered why something as simple as a short form seems different on every single site?

Some have two-column layouts with left-aligned labels. Some are right-aligned. Some are single-column with left-aligned labels above fields. Submit and Cancel buttons and the like appear on either the left or right side of the form, sometimes with the Submit button on the left of Cancel, sometimes with it on the right. And labels . . . well, don't get me started on labels.

For such simple things, there are a huge number of variants.

Sometimes, these designs are the result of pure circumstance. Maybe a designer decided that right-aligned labels simply looked better on a page, designing them to fit on the page instead of designing the page around them. Maybe a developer just threw the form together the same way he did the one on his own site. Better yet, maybe someone snagged the code from another site without bothering to modify it.

Regardless of the reason, there's a good chance the form wasn't tailored to create a good moment that contributes to the overall user experience. As a result, many forms are missed opportunities.

You may not realize it, but there are times when each variant of form layout can have a positive or negative impact on how the form (and your site) is used or perceived. And applying the right variant at the right time is one of the simplest things you can do to improve your user's experiences.

▶ Designing Forms That Flow

A form needs to flow well, and the layout of a form can play a big part in how successfully a user interacts with it. Such was the case while designing a registration form for a community site.

The form needed only to collect the user's name, email address, desired user name and password combination, and credit card information.

I considered a two-column layout with left-aligned labels.

Register

First name:	
Last name:	
Email address:	e.g. me@mydomain.com
New password:	
Confirm new password:	
Name on card:	
Card #:	
Expiration:	01 ⇕ 07 ⇕
Security code:	

OK   Cancel

This made the form nice and short, and it's likely all of it could have appeared "above the fold" on the page (in the area in view by default, without scrolling), but this layout presents a higher risk of error than other layouts do. This is because it can be difficult to map a straight line from a field label, such as Email, to its corresponding field, which appears in the second column.

The two-column layout also slows users down, which can be good if the form needs to be read carefully, but is again conducive to mistakes. With a standard registration form, it wasn't necessary to slow users down, so I considered a right-aligned version.

Register

First name:	
Last name:	
Email address:	e.g. me@mydomain.com
New password:	
Confirm new password:	
Name on card:	
Card #:	
Expiration:	01 07
Security code:	

OK   Cancel

When labels are right-aligned in a two-column layout, users make fewer mistakes than they do with left-aligned labels, because the labels and the fields are closer together. That said, right-aligned labels create an awkward, staggered edge along the left side of the page, and this lack of uniformity can be unappealing. Plus, the two-column layout still slows users down, no matter how the labels are positioned.

So I decided to plow forward with a single-column layout with top-positioned, left-aligned labels.

Register

First name:

Last name:

Email address:

e.g. me@mydomain.com

New password:

Confirm new password:

Name on card:

Card #:

Expiration:

01 ◆ 07 ◆

Security code:

OK   Cancel

This layout takes users the least amount of time to associate the labels and the fields and so they tend to move through it more quickly than they do two-column layouts. The label and field can be viewed in a single eye movement rather than the two that are required to read a label in one column and glance at a field in another. Because of this improved grouping, the single-column layout also reduces mistakes.

I use a single-column layout with top-positioned, left-aligned labels in most of the forms I design, because I always consider how the layout of a form will affect the user's moment as she interacts with it, and I often end up choosing this layout as the right solution. It's rare that I need to intentionally slow users down as they complete a form, and in such cases I usually rely on good validation techniques instead of slowing the users down. We'll talk about this more in Chapter 15.

▶Perfecting OK/Cancel

There's one more thing about even the simplest forms that can trip up users and lead to mistakes. It's that pesky OKyCancel button set that appears at the end of them.

OK and Cancel buttons are omnipresent on the Web. Of course, they aren't always labeled OK and Cancel and they don't always have the same purpose, but everyone has seen them a million times nonetheless. The combination of the two buttons has maintained its position as a global standard for a very good reason: almost any action you perform in a Web application can be canceled.

This is seen often in round-trip interactions, in which the user starts an interaction on page 1, completes it on page 2, and is then returned to page 1. It's also seen in inline interactions, such as changing the title of a Backpack page.

Typically, the set of buttons is displayed as two side-by-side buttons created with standard browser controls. Sadly, this design has persisted for years and has found its way into millions of applications.

In my form, I started with a typical OK/Cancel button set.

In this case, the object of the interaction is to register for an application. Simple enough. But there are numerous ways to solve any given design problem, and even something as simple as this requires a few decisions.

The first decision to make is about the position of the buttons. It really doesn't matter much in terms of usability whether the buttons are right-aligned or left-aligned to the field above them, but I generally stick to the left side for a few reasons.

First, left alignment keeps everything flush to the left edge, forming a nice, straight line from the top of the form to the bottom. Second—and this is simply an aesthetic choice—it seems to serve as a visual *anchor* to the form. As you complete each field, you move steadily downward. Placing the action buttons at the tail end of it seems to . . . nail everything down. But that's just me.

The second decision to make is how to label the buttons. Sure, using the standard OK and Cancel requires less effort on a case-by-case basis, because you can simply label them without really thinking about it and move on, but are these terms really helpful?

OK works fine in a lot of cases, but more meaningful button labels can go a long way toward setting a user's expectations about the result of clicking the button.

What does clicking OK do in this example? It registers the person using it as a new customer. But elsewhere in the application, OK might mean saving a configuration setting or uploading a file.

Clicking OK doesn't set a clear expectation. Fortunately, labeling the button in a meaningful way was really no big deal. All I did was change the label from OK to Register Now. Rather painless.

Primary and secondary actions

The final thing to think about here is what goes unchallenged by designers most frequently. It's the fact that *equal weight* is often given to both buttons, each of which triggers a remarkably different result. One registers the user, the other cancels the whole operation (in this case, returning the user to the home page), but the two buttons are identical in appearance.

I can understand why this apparent tradition started. Two options equates to two buttons. But what's important is not the number of options. What matters is which option is *most likely*.

The most likely option for users who have decided to register for the application and fill out this form is to click OK. This is the **primary action**. The less likely option is to cancel the registration process. This is the **secondary action**.

By giving both buttons equal visual importance, however, users have to actually read the labels—on *both* buttons—to decide which one to click.

Applying Fitts' Law, which dictates that the time it takes to hit a target is a function of the distance to the target and the size of the target, the ideal solution is to take some of the focus away from the secondary action—the Cancel button. I did this by turning it into a text link.

This way, the Register Now button is more prominent and easier to click, while the Cancel link is less prominent and slightly less easy to click.

Is it any more difficult to see both buttons? No. But it's slightly more difficult now for the user to click the wrong one. The user's eye is drawn to the large button, and it's easy to recognize, subconsciously, that the large button is the probably the primary action. If that's the one the user wants, he doesn't even need to bother reading the label. If it's the secondary action he's after, he can easily infer that the less prominent option is the Cancel link. (Ironically, creating visual separation between the two makes both easier to read, so even though users can infer their meaning without consciously reading the labels, they're now more likely to read them.)

This, incidentally, is another reason why I prefer to keep the buttons left-aligned.

Name on card:

Card #:

Expiration: Security code:
01   07

Register now   Cancel

It simply looks better to have that large HTML button aligned to the left edge of the field above it than it would to align the Cancel link to the right edge.

So, why is it helpful to keep the button on the left and the text link on the right? Because any user who uses the Tab key to move through form fields will reach the Register Now button first, again putting focus on the most likely choice while simultaneously taking focus away from the less likely choice.

It matters

Now, don't get me wrong here. A few seconds' difference in the time it takes to complete the form in each layout isn't going to make or break a user's experience. When it comes down to it, what matters is not shaving off a precious few seconds from the process, it's whether or not the value in completing the form outweighs the difficulty or tediousness of doing so.

Convincing a user to sign up in the first place is the hardest part of getting him through the registration process. But once you've accomplished this, the goal becomes to treat the user as well as possible as a customer. And considering subtle differences such as these in form design—really paying attention to the details—can result in another smooth moment for a user. And each moment contributes to the overall user experience.

If you're going to spend all the time and energy to create a Web application, why leave the design of your Web forms to chance, or to circumstance? Treat these things intentionally, and you're guaranteed to earn happier customers.

14

Conquering the Wizard

While working on an ad-campaign management system, I needed to design a form that stepped users through the campaign setup process in a particular order. They couldn't create an advertisement or set spending limits for a campaign, for example, until a campaign itself had been created, including specifying a name, start and end dates, and other criteria.

Desktop and Web applications both often contain setup processes that must be completed in a linear, step-by-step fashion. A wizard—a multistep interaction designed to walk a user through each step of a process in a predefined order—usually handles the job.

Now, any old wizard design can often do the job of helping a user complete the process, but good indicators along the way—design clues that set a user's expectations of how complicated the form might be—can increase a user's confidence and create a clear, understandable moment of interaction.

Specifically, we can set clear expectations by putting up some sign posts.

▶ Set Clear Expectations

Let's first consider what happens when a wizard lacks indicators.

Campaign setup

Campaign name:

Start date: End date:
☐ 03/03/10   ☐ 03/03/11

Geographical area:
United States ⬍

Language for the ads:
United States ⬍

(Next)

Tip:

Lorem ipsum ...

Here, the only element that tells you that you might not be finished with the interaction once this form is complete is the Next button. Nothing in the interface lets you know how many steps are part of the process of creating a campaign.

Using this design, you fill out the form and click Next. The next part of the process loads in a new page, and you fill that out and click Next again. Waiting on the other side of that Next button is yet another form. Of course, you don't know this beforehand, so each time you see another Next button, you're forced to wonder how many more steps you must complete to finish the setup process.

How far along am I? How many steps are left? How long is each step? Am I going to be filling this thing out much longer? Should I cancel my dinner plans?

Not exactly a great confidence booster.

You can easily clear up your user's frustration simply by setting her expectations—letting her know up front how many steps there are.

We should also communicate where the user has been, where she is now, and where she's going.

Campaign setup

Step 1 (of 4): **Create a campaign**

Campaign name:

Start date: End date:
☐ 03/03/10   ☐ 03/03/11

Geographical area:
United States

Language for the ads:
United States

(Next)

Tip:

Lorem ipsum ...

Doing this can be as simple as adding a descriptive title bar to each step. Here, the title bar indicates that there are four steps, the user is currently on Step 1, and Step 1 is about creating a campaign.

This alone is a big improvement, but it's not quite as helpful as it could be.

It would be incrementally more helpful to show the user the names of *all* the steps. This way, she can see at a glance what she's getting into and decide whether to continue. To do this, I tried a variation of a tab interface.

Campaign setup

| 1. Create a campaign | 2. Create an advertisement | 3. Set relevant keywords | 4. Set spending limits |

Campaign name:

Start date: End date:
☐ 03/03/10   ☐ 03/03/11

Geographical area:
United States

Language for the ads:
United States

(Next)

Tip:

Lorem ipsum ...

In this version, it's even easier to see there are four steps, and it's also easy to determine what kind of information she's going to need.

The current step is green, while the subsequent steps are disabled so the user can't access them in the wrong order. (After each step is completed, the information is stored temporarily so the next step can be validated against it.)

Establish limits

As we all know, however, there is infinite vertical space available to us on a given Web page. It doesn't matter how long a page gets, that scroll bar will just keep adjusting to let us scroll through it. Because of this, there's no way to know in this design how long each step might be.

For all you know, Step 2 contains 26 multiple-choice questions, a word puzzle, and an essay question.

I wanted to set a clearer expectation than this. I wanted users to be able to glance at the form and gather that it would take them less than five minutes to complete.

To do this, I needed to communicate that each step of the wizard was really quite short. The only way to do that was to set the area to a fixed height.

In other words, instead of tabs, I needed an accordion interface.

Campaign setup

▼ 1. Create a campaign

Campaign name:

Start date: End date:
☐ 03/03/10   ☐ 03/03/11

Geographical area:
United States

Language for the ads:
United States

Tip:

Lorem ipsum ...

Next

▶ 2. Create an advertisement

▶ 3. Set relevant keywords

▶ 4. Set spending limits

An **accordion** is the interface equivalent of the musical instrument. It consists of several panels that expand and collapse based on user input. Here, the first panel, which is **expanded** (visible or open), contains the "Create a campaign" form. The second, third, and fourth steps are in a **collapsed** (hidden or closed) state, and each of them is disabled to prevent users from accessing part of the process in an incorrect order.

With this design, the user fills out the form and clicks Next, the first panel collapses by sliding closed, and the second panel subsequently expands by sliding open. The user simply repeats this process until she reaches the end of Step 4.

Because of the fixed height, it's easy to infer that each step of the process contains a form as short or shorter than the form in Step 1. This sets the expectation that the form can be completed in a short amount of time.

Each step in the process features a Next button, just like the other designs. Step 4, however, is the final step, so instead of showing a Next button, I used a verb-noun pair.

Campaign setup

▶ 1. Create a campaign

▶ 2. Create an advertisement

▶ 3. Set relevant keywords

▼ 4. Set spending limits

Campaign daily budget (e.g. "3.00"):
$ [   ]

Max cost-per-click (e.g. "1.00"):
$ [   ]

Tip:

Lorem ipsum ...

(Save campaign)

This makes it clear that the user is saving all the information and that her campaign will now be created.

And for one last touch, I turned the title of each visited panel into a link to show users that they can return to those panels and adjust the information they entered. (Of course, some changes may affect subsequent panels. If that's the case, you can always display a message explaining the effect as soon as the user makes such a change, and then require the user to go through the next panel again.)

By showing the number of steps and providing a way to infer the length of each step, we set clear expectations for our users, so they can see what they're getting into, gauge the effort it will take to complete the process, and have yet another enjoyable, or at least relatively painless, moment.

15

Going the Extra Mile
with Inline Validation

Regardless of a form's length or complexity, one of the biggest issues with form design is the potential for error.

When we make mistakes, we blame ourselves, just as our users do. The vast majority of forms are designed with poor labels, a lack of instructive default values, and most commonly, no method of preventing and detecting mistakes. And although we may generally consider ourselves rather smart, for some reason we think it's our fault when mistakes occur instead of blaming the design of the application.

Self-blame doesn't make for a nice moment. It's exactly the opposite of what we want our users to feel when they use our products (say it with me: productive, respected, and smart).

As such, one of the best things we can do to improve an application is eliminate errors whenever possible. And since most forms are riddled with opportunities to make mistakes, they are a great place to start.

Many forms notify users of mistakes using a simple and obvious method: JavaScript alerts, like this one from GoDaddy.com's checkout process.

https://cart.godaddy.com

To register a domain you must accept the 'Domain Registration Agreement'
by checking the 'Domain Registration Agreement' checkbox on this page.

OK

Since alerts are so easy to create—all you need is one line of JavaScript—they have become the de facto standard method of reporting mistakes on the Web.

The problem is that people become so habituated to the alerts that they stop reading them, instead just passively glancing and clicking OK. It doesn't do any good to show an alert if no one reads it, or if they click OK only out of habit and not because they understand the error being reported.

Also, alerts are **application-modal,** which means that the functionality of the browser becomes disabled until the alert has been addressed. Since it's extremely rare that an error is so serious that a user absolutely must deal with the message right now, *or else,* disabling the user's browser is awfully rude. In almost every case, these errors disrupt a user's workflow for no other reason than that they're easy to create.

To keep yourself in check, keep this in mind:

The more application-modal alerts are used, the less effective they become.

They should be reserved only for emergencies, such as when a Web site is on fire and the alert can be used to break the glass and gain access to the extinguisher.

Error messages and confirmations can almost always be displayed in a much less abrasive way, creating and create a friendlier moment.

To remedy the situation while working on the checkout form for UpDown-Repeat, Kris Hadlock (a Miskeeto consultant) and I worked out solutions to eliminate as many errors as we could, and to notify users politely of others to make the form as painless as possible.

▶ Communicating Errors and Giving Kudos

On UpDownRepeat, users were asked to enter attendee and billing information to pay to attend a seminar. During this process, almost every field carried with it an opportunity for error.

A user could enter an invalid email address, miss a digit in her credit card number, skip a required field, and commit any number of other so-called mistakes.

So how could we stop the madness?

By learning from the great examples that already exist, such as Eventful's registration form.

Register

Something's wrong!
Please see the highlighted field below.

Email ⓘ

robert@miskeeto.com

Your email is for verification purposes. You will receive an email with a link for you to confirm your email address.

Username ⓘ

ro

At least 2 characters

> Username must: start with a letter; end with a letter or number; not be only numbers; and use only letters, numbers, dashes, or underscores.

Password

At least 6 characters

Not only does this form tell you something has gone wrong the second it happens, it does so through extremely noticeable red backgrounds and well-written messages.

Instead of saying, "User names must be at least 2 characters" and leaving it at that, Eventful follows up the error with more information. Specifically:

> *Username must: start with a letter; end with a letter or*
> *number; not be only numbers; and use only letters, numbers,*
> *dashes, or underscores.*

Although the message is a tad redundant—there's no need to say a username can't be all numbers when you've already said it must start with a letter—this message is helpful in explaining the options available to the user and explaining how to correct the error.

What I don't like about the Eventful form, and most forms for that matter, is that it only tells you when something is wrong, not when something is *right*. If you fill out a whole form correctly, never seeing an error message, you're still left to wonder whether or not the information has been entered correctly. You still have to wonder if you'll see a list of errors upon submitting the form.

So in addition to showing friendly error messages immediately after an error is detected, it's also nice to show users they're doing things right.

When applying these ideas to UpDownRepeat's checkout form, we started with the default state of the form.

Attendee first name: *

Attendee last name: *

Attendee email (e.g. me@mydomain.com): *

From here, we knew we wanted to let people know when they were doing things correctly, so we stole an idea from **OurProperty.co.uk**, which displays green check-mark icons next to fields that have been correctly completed after a user fills them in during their registration process.

Attendee first name: *

Robert

Attendee last name: *

Attendee email (e.g. me@mydomain.com): *

The next step, of course, was to detect errors as they occurred and to show friendly error messages to let the user know to correct them.

To do this, we created red text messages that display beneath each field. We also changed the border of the field to red to further enhance the association between the field and its error message.

Attendee first name: *

Robert   ✔

Attendee last name: *

Please enter your last name.

Attendee email (e.g. me@mydomain.com): *

Now, one of the keys to effective validation errors is to show them only *after* the user has attempted to enter something in the field. We learned this lesson from Remember the Milk, which displays an error as soon as a field gains focus.

It's fairly rude to blame a user for messing something up before she's even had the chance to enter valid information. We wanted to avoid this, so we set up these errors to display only after a field loses focus.

A question may be popping into your head right about now.

What if the user skips to the end of the form and completes something there?

In this case, a field would have never gained focus, so our error messages would not be triggered. We thought about this.

In most cases, people fill out forms in order. Because of this, it's a safe assumption this problem will almost never occur. But to ensure that users could still correct problems in this event, we created a backup plan in the form of a messaging area at the top of the page with a cream-colored background.

When and if a user skips part of the form and tries to submit the information, he sees a message like this one, listing the errors on the page.

Assuming, however, that the user sees the red error messages and corrects her entries, the errors are replaced by green check-mark icons.

No, the form is not 100 percent error-proof—I'm not even sure it's possible to accomplish that goal—but it does do an excellent job of providing constant feedback to users as they complete the form, whether the feedback is about correct entries or errors.

Updating information in real time

Finally, we wanted to make sure the total cost of the transaction was always clear and correct. To do this, we used JavaScript to update the total each time the number of attendees or of student attendees, who received a discount, changed.

By default, the user saw the standard price for the seminar.

Booking Information

Number of attendees:

1

How many of these attendees are students?

(Lowers price to $119. Make sure to bring each student's ID. They will be checked at the door.)

Promo code, if applicable:

Credit Information

Your total price of admission is: $149

If he changed the number of attendees to three, the total transaction cost changed automatically.

Booking Information

Number of attendees:

3

How many of these attendees are students?

(Lowers price to $119. Make sure to bring each student's ID. They will be checked at the door.)

Promo code, if applicable:

Credit Information

Your total price of admission is: $447

And if two of those attendees were students—changing the seminar price from $149 to $119—the total was adjusted again.

Booking Information

Number of attendees:

3

How many of these attendees are students?

(Lowers price to $119. Make sure to bring each student's ID. They will be checked at the door.)

2

Promo code, if applicable:

Credit Information

Your total price of admission is: **$387**

Between the check-mark icons, error messages, and on-the-fly updates to pricing information, this form prevented and detected almost any mistake a user could make on the form. As such, we met two goals.

First, we met the user's goal of getting through the form without a lot of hassle. Second, we met the very important *business* goal of getting people to pay for the seminar.

The best interactions are those where user goals and business goals are met simultaneously—in a pleasurable and rewarding way—with the completion of a task. A task that the user wants to complete, and is exactly what the business wants the user to do, is, well, the ideal task. The checkout process is one such task. The user doesn't necessarily want to fill out yet another form, but he wants to make a purchase so he can get his stuff. As a business, we want the user to get that same stuff, because it makes us money.

To make sure our needs are met, we need to make sure the user's needs are met. Hey—if he's going to give us money, the least we can do is help him do it, right?

Let's face it. Filling out checkout forms isn't exactly a night on the town. Doing what we can to make the process smooth ensures that the moments spent entering billing information and such are as pleasant as possible.

If we can't make it fun, we can at least make it less than awful.

16

Simplifying Long Forms

A client of mine, a gigantic insurance company, did a huge amount of research on the rules, regulations, and legalities involved in the process of applying for life insurance. Then they devised one of the most deceptive Web forms I've ever seen.

The form began as a simple group of three yes-no questions, such as "Do you, your spouse, or your dependents have any Group Medical, Dental, or Vision coverage through an Employer other than your coverage with Acme Insurance?"

If you chose the No option to each of these questions, you were safe. But if you chose Yes to any of them, the form grew. New form fields were magically inserted into the page, making it longer and requiring more effort to complete.

If you did, in fact, have coverage through an employer, check-box options for medical, dental, and vision insurance appeared. If you checked the medical option, the form grew again. The form asked for the company's name, address, and phone number. It asked for your policy number, effective date, and termination date. If you checked the dental option, the form grew again. If you checked all three, well, you were in for an afternoon of fun trying to answer questions to which you couldn't possibly know the answers.

And all this happened by choosing Yes to the *first* yes-no question. Remember, there were two others. Both produced similar results, meaning that the full length of the form was roughly three times what I've already detailed here.

What started out as a simple, three-question form quickly became a waking nightmare. The form just never ended: every time you clicked, the form grew, like that funny jelly-looking thing in *The Blob*. You could lose an entire afternoon just trying to get through the one page.

My client had good intentions—they wanted something users could fill out in a single screen, assuming that would be simpler for users. You know, because it's annoying to wait for new pages to load all the time, and it's hard to go back and fix mistakes without risking a lost session.

But something else entirely was lost while trying to complete this form. Namely, you lost all hope that you'd ever be able to complete it. Each time the form grew, your heart sank just a little more. Despair set in rather quickly. Panic came next.

Ironically, the print version of the same form was only two pages long. The Web form had simply been designed in such a way that it felt impossible to finish it.

My client wanted to know how to make it better. I requested a double-shot mocha, a full set of dry-erase markers, a giant whiteboard, and a bullwhip.

OK, I'm exaggerating. But just a little.

▶ Clear Expectations

By reducing the number of pages required to complete the form (and applying progressive disclosure in ways I didn't think were possible), my client did indeed boil the whole thing down to a single screen, but in doing so, they eliminated the user's ability to establish any sort of expectation about the process. Nothing on the page helped users determine how long they would be caught in its evil web. Instead of making it feel simpler, they made it feel complicated.

The goal shouldn't have been to create a single-screen solution. The goal should have been to trick users into believing the form was less complicated than it actually was. Not to *dupe* them, but to create the illusion of simplicity—to make the form *feel* less complicated so that the experience of filling it out was slightly less painful.

In the end, I pursued a design that set clear expectations at every step in the process to make each one more approachable and make the form as a whole feel less cumbersome than it was in reality.

First, I split the form into multiple pages and added a progress thermometer, turning the form into a wizard. Doing this meant each page could have a clear set of instructions for what paperwork was needed and let the user know how many steps were left to complete.

Second, I eliminated redundant fields to prevent users from having to enter the same information in multiple places.

The real work came, though, when trying to figure out how to set clear expectations on the first page. After all, there was no way to tell users what they were getting into without having the answers to the first few questions.

I started with the same three questions used in the original version of the form. My thinking was that the second page would be the first step of the wizard.

Do you, your spouse, or your dependents have any Group Medical, Dental, or Vision coverage through an Employer other than your coverage with Acme Insurance?

◉ Yes

◉ No

Do you, your spouse, or your dependents, have medical coverage with Medicare?

◉ Yes

◉ No

Do you, your spouse, or your dependents, have medical coverage with Medicaid?

◉ Yes

◉ No

[Get started]

I quickly realized this wasn't enough information to determine how the wizard should look. To dynamically create a wizard, I needed to know not just if the user had insurance from another provider, but whether she had medical, dental, or vision insurance. So I added check boxes to acquire this information.

Do you, your spouse, or your dependents have any Group Medical, Dental, or Vision coverage through an Employer other than your coverage with Acme Insurance?

○ Yes

    ☐ Medical   ☐ Dental   ☐ Vision

○ No

Do you, your spouse, or your dependents, have medical coverage with Medicare?

○ Yes

○ No

Do you, your spouse, or your dependents, have medical coverage with Medicaid?

○ Yes

○ No

   (Get started)

To make things a tad easier for the user, I decided that if she clicked any of these checkboxes, the Yes radio button would be selected automatically. This turned the design into a **conditional form**, in which a user's selection of one choice either enabled or disabled other form elements.

In making this decision, however, I realized there was no reason to even show the radio-button options. If the user had any of these types of insurance, the answer was obviously Yes. If the user had none, the answer was obviously No. So I removed the first set of radio buttons all together.

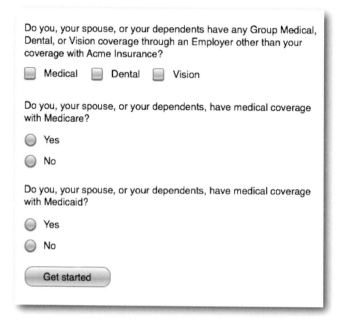

Continuing this thought, I realized there was no reason to make the user choose No for *any* of the questions. The resulting wizard process would only have sections added to it if the answer was Yes, so I decided to get rid of the rest of the radio buttons and turn the questions into check-box options.

This way, users who did not have insurance with another provider simply needed to click the Get Started button. No other action was needed. In the original design, users had to choose the No radio button for each question, so this new design required less effort.

The final trick was to tell the user what kinds of information she might need to complete the form in the first place, so she could have this information ready before she got too sucked into the process.

To do this, I added a bit of instructive text above the form, listing each of the necessary forms as bullet points, which are known to encourage quick reading.

If you have insurance through another provider, you may need to have the following information handy to complete this application:

- **Statement of coverage** *from your current insurance provider*
- **Effective dates and/or end dates** *for each type of coverage*
- **Policy numbers** *for each policy*

Other insurance

I, my spouse, or my dependents has/have Group Medical, Dental, or Vision coverage through an Employer other than your coverage with Acme Insurance. *(Choose all that apply.)*

☐ Medical   ☐ Dental   ☐ Vision

Medicare

☐ I, my spouse, or my dependents has/have medical coverage with Medicare.

Medicaid

☐ I, my spouse, or my dependents has/have medical coverage with Medicaid.

(Get started)

The new design actually looks a little less clean than it did originally, but it now requires less effort to complete, sets clear expectations from the beginning, and feels less complicated because it's broken into multiple steps.

Not all interactions can be made simple, but they can all be made to appear *easy*. By setting clear expectations and splitting complicated processes into bite-sized chunks, even the most complex interactions can feel manageable.

17
Getting Them Signed In

When I started working on Dashboard HQ with Kris Hadlock, under the partnership name 33Inc, we fully intended it to be a great tool that everyone in the world would use to manage bookmarks online. I still believe it's a great tool. But right about the time it launched, social networking became all the rage, and since our little application had no social features, it failed to pick up steam. Eventually, we lost our own steam, cut our losses, and canceled our plans to expand Dashboard HQ into a suite of productivity applications.

Regardless, the application lives on. I still use it as my browser's home page to this day, and it still does its job extremely well.

One of the things it does well is facilitate a quick sign-in process that simplifies a common pain point in most Web applications: the need to remember your user name and password.

Signing into an application is only difficult for this reason. The process of entering your user name and password is simple if you happen to know both pieces of information or set your browser to remember them for you. If neither is true, well, you might be in for an arduous process of retrieving the information you need. And doing so is usually far from enjoyable.

Many sites require you to take redundant steps to retrieve a user name or password. For example, after making several attempts to sign in using the correct user name and an *incorrect* password, eventually realizing you've just flat out forgotten your password, you click a **Forgot Password?** link and are taken to a new page, where you must then enter your user name *again*.

This happens because these systems need to know your user name before they can do anything to help you, and they don't know if the user name you entered on the Sign In page in the first place is correct. Hence, you have to enter it again. Once they know the user name, they usually either send the existing password to you by email, or send you a link to another page on the site through which you will create a new password.

Quite a hassle, no?

While attempting to improve on this old standard and come up with something a little more enjoyable, we asked ourselves a simple question.

What if the system already knew your user name?

▶ Improving on Standards, Again

If the system already knew your user name, you wouldn't need to enter it on a second page to tell the system to send your lost password to you. The system could do this immediately, without any extra effort on your part. And since the Lost Password page would be unnecessary, your lost password could be emailed to you with a single click.

User name vs. a user's name

To make this idea a reality, we designed the system so that the user name is part of the URL the user uses to sign into the application.

So, instead of bookmarking the home page, the user bookmarks his own personal Sign In page. If his user name is john, he signs in at www.dashboardhq.com/john. If he tries to access the page and he is signed in already, he is automatically redirected to his Dashboard HQ page. If not, he signs in using just his password.

If the user happens to share a computer with other people and suddenly finds himself staring at a Sign In page that doesn't belong to him, a small link is offered that simply states, "I am not John." When clicked, the displayed user name is converted into an input field so he can enter his user name.

The idea here is pretty simple. Why require a frequent user to remember his user name when we can remember it for him?

Instead of forcing users to complete a Username field like every other Sign In page in the known world, we offer something a little extra to ease the pain of remembering user names.

And since we already know the user name, when a user clicks the <u>Forgot Password?</u> link, we don't need to send him to another screen to reenter it. Instead, clicking the link simply sends an email containing the password to the email address we have on file for that user name, and we display a simple message on the Sign In page letting the user know the password was sent.

Above and beyond

The folks who designed the IxDA (Interaction Design Association) site, used as a home for the IxDA's rather active discussion list, took their desire to simplify Sign In processes even further.

In fact, the site doesn't even require a password.

Your Name

Robert

Subscription E-mail

robert@miskeeto.com

Sign In <u>What about passwords?</u>

All you do is enter your name and the email address you used to register for the site. If you can't remember the version of your name you used when you registered—first name only, first *and* last name, or some other combination—fret not. The site uses your email address as the primary identification method, and matches any version of your name to the record in the database.

For example, I registered using the name Robert Hoekman, Jr., but if I type only *Robert* into the Your Name field, I can still sign in. And if I type in a name I didn't use, like Joe, I get an error message.

This name and e-mail address do not match. Please use the name you're known by on the IxDA discussion list.

Your Name

Joe

Subscription E-mail

robert@rhjr.net

Sign In   What about passwords?

This makes me feel slightly more secure about my account in the absence of a password, but what happens if I enter the name and email address for another list member? I know quite a few members, so this would be easy to do. Can I simply log in and start posting as that person?

Um, no. When I try to do this, a message is displayed that states that I've never used this computer or network to sign in before, so a confirmation request is being sent to the email address I entered.

Oops. I hope the guy whose email address I used to test out the functionality doesn't think I was trying to hack his account.

The IxDA solution wouldn't be appropriate for every application: it's not as secure as a site that requires at least a password.

Also, entering a user name is such a common habit that some people who log into the site find themselves entering what they guess is their user name into the Your Name field, when what they really need to type is their actual name. Deviating from what is normally a habit can make the simplified Sign In process require more thought than a traditional design. Especially since there's no way to know that you can enter any variation of your name you want. This forces users to wonder if they need to enter their name exactly as they did when they registered for the site.

But aside from these issues, the IxDA Sign In process is a great attempt to raise the bar for other designers. The designers are actively questioning standards to see not *if* but *how* they can be improved.

Standards are never written in stone. In fact, most of the time, they change the second after someone bothers to write them down. Taking a fresh look at anything normally considered old hat is a great way to elevate the user experience of any application.

18
Counting Characters

In billiards, there are a few different ways to win a game. The most reliable way is to spend a whole lot of time perfecting your stroke, tweaking your stance, becoming a master strategist, and practicing the tough shots as diligently as the easy ones. This is what the pros do. They spend years running drills, playing against people better than they are, and pushing themselves to be great.

A less reliable but still effective way is to learn the basics of stroke, stance, and strategy, and become a decent player who can hold your own. No professional pool-playing aspirations here. Just a solid ability to beat most people who challenge you on a bar table.

The least reliable method is the one most people learn and subsequently stick to. It's the poke-and-hope method. This means you poke your pool cue at that little white ball and hope something goes into a pocket.

Beginners almost always rely on poke-and-hope. More advanced players occasionally find themselves in situations where they need to rely on it as well. Pros do it the least, but it still happens.

In the same way that most pool players fall into the beginner category, most computer users never learn the basic concepts and techniques for using a computer effectively. This happens, of course, because they have better things to do than master the personal computer, just like they have better things to do than become master pool players.

Regardless, this leads to all sorts of problems. People right-click in Web applications and look for task-level options in the browser's default context menu. They enter their email addresses into the browser's Address bar and wonder why their email doesn't come up. They hold a piece of paper up to a monitor screen and wonder why it can't be scanned. And more often than not, they click a Submit button at the bottom of a form and pray they filled it out correctly so they don't see a bunch of annoying error messages that will make them feel stupid.

In other words, they poke and hope.

If you're a poke-and-hope kind of pool player, you may be able to empathize with how most people feel when working with software on the Web. There's no skill, no foundation, no deep knowledge. There's only the hope that whatever you poke will get you one step closer to stealing a game or two.

The cure for a lot of this is poka-yoke (more on this below).

Eliminating the possibility of error in your application means your poke-and-hope users can now use your application without feeling like morons, even if they know next to nothing about how the Web really works. Even if they think Internet Explorer's Help menu contains information about your Web application. Even if they enter URLs into the search box on your site in hopes that the new site will magically appear.

The single best thing you can do to significantly improve your Web applications—now and forever—is remove the possibility of error. Users who can't make mistakes feel smart. They feel respected. They feel productive.

Smart, respected, productive users are the best users in the whole world, because they tell other people how great it is to use your application. And that's just good marketing.

If you want people to talk about *your* application like this, the best way to start is to turn poke-and-hope into poka-yoke.

I attempt to do this with the design of every application I work on, so I had loads of examples to choose from when I sat down to write this chapter. I settled on an example of a common problem: input fields with character limits.

▶ Reaching Your Limits

Every so often a form field requires a character limit. This can happen with Create Password fields, for example, when passwords can only be up to eight or ten characters long.

Whenever I need to create a form field with a character limit, I do it pretty much the same way. This is because when I did this the first time, I went on a road trip through various Web sites and studied all the implementations I could find, made notes about how they worked, and devised what I thought was the best solution. And I've yet to find a case where this solution wasn't appropriate.

I know, I know, you're wondering why I bother obsessing over such simple and mundane details, right? This is not a difficult interface issue, after all, and it's hardly worth any real thought.

But before you pass judgment, consider some of the restricted fields you've encountered in the past.

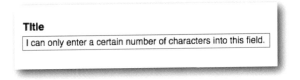

In some restricted fields, you enter a complete text string, submit the form, and then see a message like this.

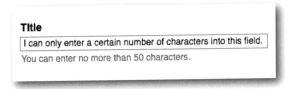

This limitation, of course, forces you to manually count the characters you've entered to see how many you must trim to comply with the restriction. And this is a tedious, awful thing to have to do. And you resent it. And since you don't know if spaces count against you, you still can't feel confident that your count is going to be accurate.

In another common implementation, you start happily typing along and eventually notice that your keyboard has . . . well, it looks like it has broken.

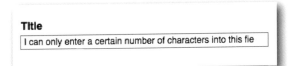

You typed out a whole novella only to find out that the last 200 characters were never entered into the field. In an effort to find out what went wrong, maybe you type something into another application open on your desktop to make sure your keyboard is still working. Or maybe—and yes, I've done this myself—you check behind your computer to make sure the USB cable for your keyboard is still plugged in.

And just like that, an ordinary input field makes you think your whole computer is on the fritz.

Sad.

Is this really the kind of moment you want to create for your users? I didn't think so. Fortunately, this problem is ridiculously simple to fix.

Poka-yoke in editing

All that's needed is a simple way to let users know what's going on. First, to let them know that there is a character limit, and second, to let them know when they've reached it.

Poka-yoke to the rescue! As I discussed in *Designing the Obvious,* **poka-yoke** is the Japanese term for "error-proofing," and there are two types of poka-yoke devices: **detection** devices and **prevention** devices. I love finding ways to apply this idea to the Web.

A detection device is anything that lets a user know an error has occurred and enables him to correct it immediately. Error messages of *any* kind are poka-yoke detection devices.

A prevention device, however, is something that prevents an error from occurring in the first place. And restricted fields are a great place to put the idea into action.

The simplest solution is to add a bit of instructive text that explains to users that there is a limit of 50 characters.

TItle

I can only enter a certain number of characters into this fie

Enter up to 50 characters.

This lets a user know about the limit so she doesn't wonder why her keyboard stopped working. But without something to tell her when she's reached the character limit, she still has to count characters as she goes:

"'I can only enter' . . . let's see . . . that's 13 characters, so . . . I have 37 left. OK . . . 'a certain number' . . . wait, how many is that now? And do spaces count? Oof. This sucks."

To turn this instructive text into a poka-yoke device, I changed the number 50 in the text into a decrementing variable.

Now, as the user types, the number decreases with each added character. The user knows exactly how many characters can still be entered the whole time she types into the field. And, of course, the number increases whenever a character is deleted.

When she gets to zero, she can adjust her entry much more effectively.

After putting this design together, I immediately made it the standard for my employer at the time and wrote up a blog post about it.

It was then pointed out to me that there was a small problem with the design.

Because screen readers read pages in chronological order, a person using one wouldn't see the message about the character limit until *after* he had finished typing.

Silly me.

To remedy this, I simply moved the message with the decrementing variable above the field, like so.

Title
You can enter up to 33 more characters.

I can only enter a cer

Now, it's true that a person using a screen reader will have to periodically Shift > Tab his way back to the message to see how many characters are left, but at least now he'll know about the restriction before he starts typing, and he has a method for checking the current character count.

A little extra warning

Incidentally, the Twitter Web site takes character counter design even further. The decrementing variable starts out as gray text, but as soon as a user enters more than 120 characters, the number changes to red to let her know she has fewer than 20 characters left available.

Nice touch.

This way, even if the user doesn't notice the text initially, the color change is likely to get her attention as she types. Red stands out against everything else on most Web pages, and the sudden appearance of red often breaks a user's concentration long enough to make her notice the character counter.

The only problem I have with the design is that the character counter has no associated text or label to explain what it means.

What are you doing?   85

Wondering why Twitter's character counter has no label.

(update)

Regardless, the addition of a simple character counter is all it takes to turn a potential mistake into another "All it takes to use this application is pure common sense" moment for your users.

Instead of forcing users to count characters manually or letting them make the mistake of entering too many before seeing an error message, this simple addition makes the interaction obvious.

PART V

Participating

Participation is the fun part of using the Web.

It's when we go from being passive explorers to connecting with other people, managing and editing information about ourselves and others, sharing ideas, making plans, and generally having a lot of fun.

And there's a huge number of ways to join in the fun on the Web these days. The rise of social media has made it possible for us to do everything from play poker with a kid in Japan to stay in constant communication with a spouse who's 1,000 miles away on a business trip.

But regardless of whether users are writing a comment on a blog post, making virtual friends on Facebook, or designing a Web page of their own through a Web site builder tool, these moments are filled with the potential for confusion and lost confidence.

In this part, I tell some stories about participatory features and talk about a few principles that can help you make these moments understandable and positive for your own users.

Over the next six chapters, I talk about why clarity is more important than efficiency, how to encourage social interactions, and even why following a person's activities on a site can be more appropriate than becoming their "friend."

Whatever the underlying purpose, even the most complicated interactions can become enjoyable moments.

19

Building Profiles

While working on the graphic artist community site I discussed in Chapter 1, one of the challenges was to come up with a user profile system that was more meaningful than a simple page of facts about a site member.

What I did was nothing revolutionary, or even new, but it serves as a good example of how the type of application being created can affect the types of information members need about other users.

A user profile is often comprised of a few vital statistics about a person—his name, Web site URL, instant messenger information, and maybe a list of hobbies or a short blurb about why he joined the site. This information isn't always particularly helpful to the other site members, because it isn't designed to contribute to a user's image of another person in any meaningful way. Still, it often makes a new user feel warm and fuzzy enough that he'll spend his otherwise valuable time entering these details.

In this community of graphic artists, however, we knew there were a couple of different types of users—artists, and people in need of art (buyers). And we knew that, very often, a user would want to learn more about another user's favorite galleries, comments, and uploaded galleries to see if it would lead them to more good content. For example, Josh could see a gallery he likes, and then wish to see other galleries from the same artist. Likewise, Josh could notice that a gallery was rated highly by Sarah, another buyer, and wish to see a list of other galleries Sarah liked.

To meet these needs, we first **layered** the profile creation process, then we designed a profile page that grew dynamically to become a **dashboard**—a living record of a user's site activity.

Let me explain.

▶ Progressive Enhancements

Every user who decided to sign up on the site was asked to complete standard profile information. This included the user's name, email address, password, and credit card information.

Graphic artists, however, could do a whole slew of things on the site that other members wouldn't need to do, such as create galleries of their work, list their rates and availability for contract work, and specify their areas of expertise.

To handle this, we took a **layered** approach. We asked anyone creating a gallery for the first time to enter extra information that would be added to his profile. The information only applied to artists who were attempting to market themselves through the site.

Sign out | **My Account** | Contact Us | Help

Artist, category, project, etc.

Search

My Account

Inbox (5)
Projects (2)
Bids (14)
My Profile

Create a gallery
Write journal entry
Visit the forums
etc...

Tell us about your services
This information will appear as part of your profile from now on.

Rate and availability
Rate:

$0.00   per hour

Availability:

Contract only

How soon could you start a new project?

In one week

Your specialties:
Enter as many as you want.

Graphic design

Add another specialty

Additional comments
Tell us more about yourself:

Save   Cancel

Because only graphic artists using the site would need to enter this information, we left it out of the registration process. Simply put, we didn't want every last person who registered to feel they had to be a graphic artist to sign up.

People looking to contract a graphic artist for a project or simply explore the site for inspiration would never see the form for entering additional profile information.

From data to dashboard

Regardless of the type of user—artist, buyer, or fan—the software automatically creates a profile page for each member that can be viewed by any other site member.

As a user starts taking action on the site, the profile page is updated to reflect the person's activities.

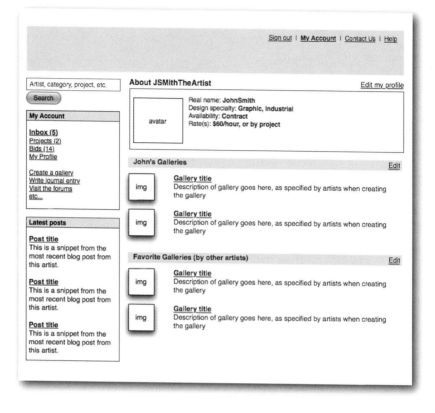

So, as John the Artist creates a gallery to show off his work, marks a few other galleries as his favorites, lists his availability and rates for contract work, writes journal entries, and so on, his profile page is updated to show this information.

Any site member can explore another member's profile to see what galleries he likes, see what galleries he's created himself or commented on, and read his journal entries.

The profile page, then, becomes much more than a page of vital stats. It becomes a living record of a member's activity on the site.

There are several major benefits here. First, whenever you find a gallery you like, you can click to see other galleries from the same person. Second, when you see a comment or high rating from another site member who appears to have impressions similar to your own, you can click to see what other galleries the person liked and what he's said about *those*.

In other words, you can use any site member's profile page as an aggregate portal to good content. If you know that Sarah the Buyer has liked many of the same things you have liked, you can start repeat experiences on the site by jumping to Sarah's profile to see what she's been checking out most recently.

The blank slate

If a user registers as a site member but never takes any additional action, his profile page is treated as a **blank slate**.

A blank slate is any page devoid of the data that will eventually fill it up. Since the user has yet to do anything on the site—such as mark a gallery as a favorite—the user's profile page is relatively empty.

The best thing to do with blank slates is use them to encourage people to take action. In this case, a profile page with no profile information to list instead offers links to explore featured galleries, create a gallery, and so on. This way, the uninitiated user is further encouraged to start creating his own gallery or posting.

Profiles often comprise just a few simple personal details about a user, but profiles can also present an opportunity. In cases like this one, profiles can become an effective social communication device that provides a clear pathway to useful information about other members' likes and dislikes.

By providing this information, a user can begin to *trust* members with similar tastes and seek them out on return visits to see what else they've recently explored. And with this trust comes a reason to return to the site over and over again.

20

Editing

Back in Chapter 3, I talked about redesigning the navigation for a Web site builder application. In this chapter, I want to talk about another issue in the same application—the editing functionality, which needed a lot more work than a few tweaks to menus.

See, this application suffered from a bad case of *featuritis*. In scientific terms, featuritis is a disease of poor usability caused by the inclusion of far too many features in an application. (OK, so it's not exactly scientific.)

In this case, the boatload of features that had been crammed into the application were making for an unwieldy user experience. And the editing functionality—the most essential and most often used functionality in the application—suffered greatly as a result.

Whenever a user attempted to perform an editing task, for example, such as formatting text in a text block or adding an image to the Web page he was designing, a popup window opened. Almost every interaction involved dealing with this pesky popup window.

The popup window contained tools for formatting text, editing images, inserting time stamps, creating RSS feeds . . . you name it, it was there.

Naturally, I wondered why all this functionality couldn't exist in the main window, eliminating the need for the popup. But I also wondered why users had to dig their way through every possible available tool while trying to find the one they actually needed at a given moment.

For example, to format text, the user had to move his mouse to the text block, choose Edit from a small menu that appeared when rolling over the block, and wait for the popup window to launch and render. When that was complete, he had to select the text he wanted to edit, and then look through several rows of toolbar icons to find the formatting option he wanted (Bold, for example). After applying the formatting change, he had to click a Save button, wait for the popup window to close, and then wait for the text block in the original window to update.

If he wanted to format another bit of text, he had to do it all over again. If he wanted to undo the change, his only option was to follow the same steps.

This process, as you can imagine, got *really* tedious after just a few modifications to the Web page being designed. These were not pleasant moments, by any means.

And the two rounds of usability testing we did confirmed this belief. Our testers, some of whom had previous experience with the application, were frustrated when it came to completing even the most basic tasks.

With all the editing tools remaining available 100% of the time in the very messy popup window, it was difficult at best to find the ones a user needed to complete the task at hand. There were probably a couple hundred different tools and options in this single popup window, but only three or four applied to any particular task. When formatting text, for example, the icon for inserting a calendar into your Web page was not helpful. To the contrary, it got in the way of the user's interaction goal. Most of the tools in the popup window were unrelated to the most common tasks.

And the fact that all these tools were in a popup window in the first place meant that users were trying to edit Web page elements out of context of the page itself. They couldn't see the page they were editing and edit it at the same time, because the popup window got in the way.

Due to a lack of resources, there was never an interaction designer assigned to the product prior to my taking it on. The developers did their best (despite the constant requests of users and internal executives to add more and more functionality), always trying to make decisions that kept users' interests in mind. Without a deep understanding of how to make a product usable, however, and without a long-term plan for how the application would evolve, the development team eventually ended up having to crowbar new features into place. And since they were never allowed the time to clean things up and set a more effective course of action, the developers were trapped. All they could do was tack new features onto the interface wherever they could, and hope for the best.

They'd heard all the same complaints about the application I had, and they were just as tired of it as I was. Fortunately, we managed to win the support of a few key executives, and were able to get the ball rolling on a redesign.

We started with the editing features.

Cleaning up the mess wasn't easy. It took several days worth of whiteboard sessions and conversations with the other designers on my team, as well as developers on the project, to come up with a solution that was both technically feasible and would solve some of the most significant usability issues.

▶ The Right Tools at the Right Time

In the interest of alleviating much of the confusion with the editing features, we knew we wanted to show only the tools that were relevant to a task as it was being performed, and we wanted users to be able to edit their Web pages *directly* instead of taking them away from the page to edit on another screen.

In doing this, our hope was to make the application, which was overloaded with features, *appear* very simple. By showing only the relevant tools at the appropriate moment, each task would seem easy, despite that the application was so robust.

We started by moving all the functionality out of the popup window and into the main window, right alongside the Web page being edited. This solved the context issue, but we were a long way from solving the bigger problem.

How would we hide the tools and options that were irrelevant to a task?

We considered simply disabling tools that could not be used, but this meant users couldn't change their minds mid-stream. For example, if image-editing tools were disabled when a text block was selected, a user who decided to edit some text couldn't change her mind and insert an image instead.

So, we knew we had to make sure that all the tools were available all of the time, while hiding the irrelevant tools at the same time.

We considered a design similar to the Properties panel design used in many Adobe products, such as this one from Adobe Flash.

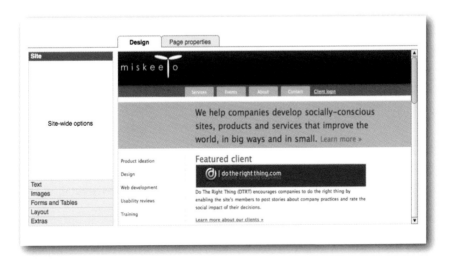

Here, the panel options change based on which tool is currently in use. (These are Text Tool options.)

This would let us show options relevant to the task being performed, but we couldn't fill up the screen with a bunch of tool panels, so the design left us without a way to keep all the *other* tools available.

Fortunately, we'd used accordion designs, like the one discussed in Chapter 14, in several other applications around the same time we were on this project, and we thought to explore it as an option. (I'm showing only the accordion and the Web page editing area here in the interest of keeping the images legible. To show the whole application, we'd need a larger book.)

In this very rough draft, the whole idea was that we could surface the most common tools and options in the accordion panels, and have the appropriate panel open automatically based on the action being performed by a user.

For example, when a user clicked on a text block, the Text panel would open.

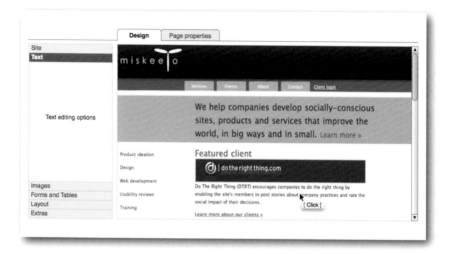

This panel would offer formatting options, such as Bold, Italic, Underline, and so on. It would also include a menu for choosing a font, font size, and font color.

These were the right tools at the right time. When a user clicked a text block to either write, edit, or format text, these were the tools that needed to be handily available.

Clicking on an image would open the Images panel and offer options to edit its dimensions. Clicking on a blank area in the Web page being edited would open the Site panel, which would offer options that applied to the whole site, such as Create Page and Organize Navigation.

We spent a couple of days figuring out which tools would be available in each panel, and how we would provide access to tools not in the panels.

The solution was a simple matter of applying the principle of progressive disclosure.

Hiding the advanced stuff

As discussed in Chapters 11 and 16, **progressive disclosure** is a method for progressively revealing features based on how common or necessary they are.

In this case, surfacing only the tools relevant to a task was the right thing to
do, but we still needed a way to offer the rest of the tools and options in those
cases where they were needed.

So, we established a design for document-modal dialog boxes that would
contain additional options. By **document-modal**, I mean that the dialog box
would temporarily prevent interaction with the Web page being edited—the
Edit pane—but users would still be able to interact with other parts of the
application and the browser itself.

For example, when a user clicks a text block and the Text panel opens, this
panel includes an option to convert selected text into a link. But we couldn't
stick all of the options for links inside the accordion panel, so we moved those
into a dialog box.

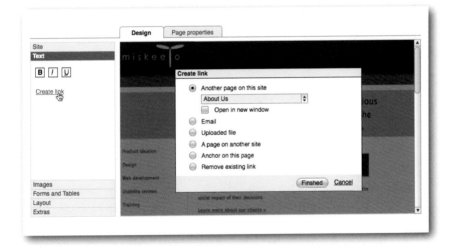

So, the Edit pane is dimmed out and disabled, and this dialog box opens within
the same screen area. Within the dialog box, you choose link options and click
the Finished button to create the link.

The *trigger* for the interaction—the **Create a link** option—appears in the accordion panel, but the options for the feature are presented in a dialog box.

Cleaning up

As of this writing, the application is still being worked on. Functionally, it's still fairly slow and heavy—it's a big job, after all—but an overhaul of the design of the editing features improved the usability of the application quite a bit.

The fact is, when there is an overwhelming number of tools and options with which to accomplish tasks in an application, sometimes the best you can do is take a fresh look at what's there and see how it can be improved. In this case, progressive disclosure was the key to surfacing only the tools and options that were needed for each task.

The key is to show the right tools at the right time. This way, the decisions that need to made by users and the steps required to complete common tasks are dramatically reduced, making each interaction easier to perform, and each interaction *moment* incrementally more enjoyable.

21
Making Social Connections

Ah, friends. We laugh together, cry together, goof off together—these are the people with whom we choose to spend our increasingly precious and valuable time when we're away from our computers.

But friendships formed online through social media sites like Facebook, MySpace, LinkedIn, Twitter, and many others aren't *quite* the same as the friendships we form offline.

Online friendships are often contrived and artificial. Sure, we can connect with our *real* friends, assuming they're using the same sites, but very often, we **friend** people we don't know. These can be people we meet through forums, discussion lists, friends of other friends, people we respect and admire but haven't met in person, and so on.

And sadly, there is often little meaning or depth to these friendships. Take Facebook, for example. When you friend someone on Facebook, their activities are listed on your Facebook page. But their activities are frequently related to friending *other* people, giving virtual gifts, writing messages, and so on. Sure, it's fun, but in the end you're left with a whole lot of noise and not a whole lot of signal. It can be endlessly entertaining, but also quite purposeless, at least in practical terms.

As such, friending is an activity, like any other, that is best reserved for the right circumstances.

Friending is the cornerstone of Facebook, MySpace, and other sites, but there are plenty of contexts in which friending makes no sense at all.

When the guys at DoTheRightThing decided to explore the addition of friending to the site, I suspected it could be one of those cases.

DTRT's purpose is to raise awareness of both ethical and unsavory behavior on the part of corporations. This isn't necessarily a fun activity. It's a socially conscious behavior, sure, which can be fun and fulfilling, but it's not like going clubbing on a Friday night.

The basic idea was that, as on many other social sites, users would have the ability to friend another site member via the member's profile page. A user visiting the page would simply click the Become My Friend button, and a lasting, meaningful bond would immediately form between the two people. They would meet for a neighborhood poker game on Friday nights, and their sons would become best friends, attend the same schools, and eventually marry two sisters in a joint hillside wedding.

OK, so I didn't quite understand the purpose of friending on DTRT.

My first question was, So what happens when you become someone's friend?

Turns out, the idea was very new, so no one had really fleshed it out yet. They knew they wanted to encourage people to check out more stories on the site—members were often checking out just one story, rating it, and leaving—and they figured that offering a way to connect with other people was a good incentive.

I thought they were onto something with the initial concept, but it needed some tuning.

▶ Friends vs. Followers

Facebook offers myriad ways to keep up with a friend's activities, as does MySpace. But most of these features and activities are rendered all but useless on a site like DTRT, where the focus is on social change and not on entertainment.

Adding a friending feature to DTRT would look something like this.

Robert's Profile

Robert Hoekman, Jr.
34 year old male from Arizona

Website: http://miskeeto.com

About Me
Doing the right thing for 8 months
Consectetuer adipiscing elit, sed diam nonummy nibh euismod tincidunt ut laoreet dolore magna aliquam erat volutpat. Ut wisi enim ad minim veniam, quis nostrud exerci tation ullamcorper suscipit lobortis nisl ut aliquip ex ea commodo consequat. Duis autem vel eum iriure dolor in hendrerit in vulputate velit esse molestie consequat, vel illum dolore eu feugiat nulla facilisis at vero eros.

[**Become my friend!**]

My Friends

See all 46 friends

How I'm Doing the Right Thing

Today

Ryan found my story "Universal to test selling DRM-free music" about Universal Music Group important

Rod found my story "Universal to test selling DRM-free music" about Universal Music Group important

My friend Robert found my story "Universal to test selling DRM-free music" about Universal Music Group important

I posted the story "Universal to test selling DRM-free music"
about Universal Music Group

2 days ago

Robert is now friends with Mike Hill.

Robert is now a friend!

John is now a friend!

My friend Ryan posted the story "New program fights global warming" about Virgin Group

My friend Ryan added the company BioCyte International

Ryan is now a friend!

Rod is now a friend!

And this is exactly how we started. There was a button to click to become someone's friend, a collection of profile images of the member's friends, and a link to see the whole list of friends.

But this picture wasn't gelling with the nature of DTRT, so Rod Ebrahimi and I passed wireframes back and forth for a few days by email and talked quite a bit about the nature of friendships online and how the whole idea might fit into DTRT.

We came up with very few answers.

What would happen when someone clicked the Become My Friend button? What activities would be built into the site to encourage these friendships? Would these things really encourage members to read and post more stories?

No matter how we looked at it, friending functionality simply didn't make sense for DTRT.

What we really wanted wasn't friendship, but a simple and unobtrusive feature that would encourage people to read more posts and get more involved.

In the end, we followed Twitter's lead.

Twitter offers a low-effort friending solution called **following**. Simply put, any site member can follow another member's Twitter feed by simply going to her profile page and clicking Follow.

No effort is required beyond that, and all that results is the ability for a member to keep up with the activities of another member. That's all there is to it.

We thought that the simple act of following someone's activities sounded more appropriate for DTRT. By scanning a list of stories posted by the people I'm following and the names of the people those people are following, you can quickly spot interesting stories, find out who has rated which story as important, and so on.

Strangely, all it took to remedy the situation was a few tweaks to the text in the left-hand sidebar. (These changes hadn't been built yet, because no one knew what to build. Using wireframes, we were able to make and change these decisions before getting into the heavy lifting of writing code.)

We changed the button label from Become My Friend to Follow My Activities, and then changed the surrounding text to match this tone. Instead of a "My Friends" heading for other members' profile images, we used "Who's Following Me?" Instead of a link to "See all 46 friends," we used "See all 46 followers."

These simple changes brought the picture together nicely. Now, a DTRT member could simply glance at a profile page and see an aggregate list of a whole bunch of other people's activities on the site. In theory, this would encourage them to read more stories on the site and subsequently post more of their own.

Not present at time of photo

As of this writing, these changes have not been built out and added to the site, so I can't say at the moment whether we made the right decision or not. But since we took a good look at the problem and made decisions based on those insights, we believe the site will be all the better as a result, and we'll be able to offer DTRT members something that is right for them.

I know that social media is all the rage on the Web these days, but the functionality that so often comes with social media—friending, ratings, reviews, and so on—all need to be carefully considered before simply being thrown into yet another snap-together social networking site. The same is true for Ajax, DHTML, Adobe Flash, and any new craze that comes along.

Don't let the hype get to you. Think before you leap.

22

Designing the Obvious Blog

When I designed the blog template I'm about to show you, I had no client. In fact, I had no design software, no whiteboard, no chalkboard, no pen, no paper, and *no idea* what I was about to do.

Here's the story.

In July 2007, I spoke at WordCamp, which is a single-room, one-session-at-a-time annual event put on by Automattic, the makers of WordPress, during which WordPress bloggers come together for two days of sessions and conversation focused entirely on blogs.

When I arrived, I was prepared to give a presentation based on my book, *Designing the Obvious.* I'd given the session several times before and felt pretty confident with it, and I had tweaked my slide deck to focus more on blogs, somehow thinking this would satisfy my audience. But after watching a couple of the presentations that came before mine, I realized the audience I was about to talk to couldn't care less about the guiding principles of Web application design.

I was about to get up in front of 300 or so people and completely bomb. And I had about an hour to avert the impending crisis.

I ducked out to the lobby, opened up my laptop, and quickly perused my slides. I made some tweaks and tried desperately to convince myself I could get away with giving the session as it was.

Who was I kidding?

I closed my slide deck, opened up a text-editing application, and started writing notes about what I thought made for a good blog design.

About 30 minutes later, I got up on stage and told the very energetic crowd that I had scrapped my presentation and would be showing them no slides whatsoever. They applauded. Apparently they didn't like slides.

For the next hour, I led a discussion, not a presentation, on good blog design. I talked about some of the principles from the book, asked open-ended questions about how the principles had been applied to blog designs, and asked how we could further improve blog designs based on the same ideas.

Fortunately, the crowd went with me on this journey. They were loud, involved, engaged, and enthusiastic. They shouted out great ideas. They argued with each other from across the room. They were amazing!

As we talked, I kept a running mental list of all the things we collectively decided would make for a great blog design. Toward the end of the session, I summed up the points, mentioned my book one last time, and got the heck offstage.

A few hours later, I opened up OmniGraffle and created a wireframe based on the conversation.

▶ Three Ways to a Better Blog

There were three primary points that came out of the talk.

First, we decided—or perhaps *realized*—that blogs should make it easier for site visitors to scan a page to determine whether or not a post is worth reading.

Newspaper articles are written so that the first couple of sentences reveal high-level information that tells readers what the story is about. Blogs, however, are not typically written by journalists, and as such, they very rarely offer rock-solid opening statements that summarize the remainder of the post. But when we visit a blog, this is the first thing we want to see.

Second, we decided that blogs should do a better job of encouraging conversation. Most blogs offer the ability for users to add comments, but we believed more can be done to encourage conversation than simple commenting.

The most obvious method is to offer "trackbacks." Trackbacks, as you may know, are snippets from articles that appear on a post page, aggregated from other sites that reference the post. The problem is that very few blogs explain what trackbacks are or how they work. And if only other knowledgeable bloggers are able to leverage the technology, the potential for viral, multisite conversation becomes very limited.

Finally, we decided that a good blog design should entice people to read more posts. This is because when we visit a site to read a blog post, we often stay on the site only long enough to read that post. We don't stick around to learn more about the site, the author, or the organization that maintains the blog.

Suggestions from the crowd included offering links to related posts, most popular posts, and other post categories. There should also be links to the previous and next post (if applicable).

Another solution is to offer an RSS feed. And because most people have no idea what *RSS* means or what it can do for them, the button that links to the feed should be labeled Subscribe or the like—something that will make sense to people who aren't geeks.

And as I discussed in *Designing the Obvious,* the RSS subscription page should contain a short explanation of RSS, offer links to several RSS reader applications, and be formatted in a presentable way instead of offering a page full of XML.

Of course, we also thought that blog templates should contain all the usual stuff, such as the authors' names (if the blog had multiple contributors), the date a post was written, links to other sections of the site, a Search bar, and other common elements.

The solutions

The net result of our conversation was this wireframe.

The Obvious Blog

Short blog description goes here to provide context to users who land on this page and have no idea what they're looking at.

| Search |

Subscribe

A provocative post title goes here

Short summary of this post, so users can quickly determine if it's worth reading.

In this site

Main nav link
Main nav link
Main nav link
Main nav link

Next post
Some post title

Previous post
Some post title

Lorem ipsum dolor sit amet, consectetuer adipiscing elit. Maecenas vulputate sodales dolor. Lorem ipsum dolor sit amet, consectetuer adipiscing elit. Phasellus in arcu. Cras sem urna, gravida eget, facilisis a, vulputate eget, arcu. Quisque mi diam, cursus a, dapibus non, ornare nec, mi. Fusce et nunc vitae mi porta imperdiet. Etiam non quam. Pellentesque tortor. Duis vestibulum velit et lectus. Etiam aliquet semper sapien. Class aptent taciti sociosqu ad litora torquent per conubia nostra, per inceptos hymenaeos.

Categories

Current category
Category link
Category link
Category link
Category link
Category link
Category link
Category link
Category link

Related posts

Related post link
Related post link
Related post link
Related post link

Vivamus faucibus. Proin ante libero, auctor a, accumsan sit amet, sollicitudin eget, massa. Praesent diam. Suspendisse interdum eleifend odio. Nulla nec arcu. Sed tincidunt pretium orci. Cras justo nulla, iaculis lacinia, vulputate in, aliquam vel, felis. Sed sit amet nisl. Duis commodo nonummy est. In posuere elit at turpis. Praesent euismod aliquam nulla. Praesent dictum, orci sit amet sagittis euismod, lacus mauris pulvinar ligula, vel lacinia diam nulla vitae turpis. Nulla est nulla, sollicitudin ut, vulputate a, nonummy sit amet, risus. Sed dolor nisl, pretium sit amet, placerat eget, rutrum vitae, justo. Pellentesque turpis lectus, varius at, sodales ac, rutrum vel, metus. Phasellus sed metus. Nulla rutrum quam in velit. Mauris et enim in ipsum congue ultrices. Suspendisse eget turpis.

Popular posts

Popular post link
Popular post link
Popular post link
Popular post link

Posted by Robert on October 3, 2007

What others sites are saying

Link to the following address from your own site, and this page will list your article: http://www.mydomain.com/post/trackback

From somedomain.com:

"Lorem ipsum dolor sit amet, consectetuer adipiscing elit. Maecenas vulputate sodales dolor."

From somedomain.com:

"Lorem ipsum dolor sit amet, consectetuer adipiscing elit. Maecenas vulputate sodales dolor."

3 comments (Subscribe to comments)

Someone said:

Lorem ipsum dolor sit amet, consectetuer adipiscing elit. Maecenas vulputate sodales dolor. Lorem ipsum dolor sit amet, consectetuer adipiscing elit. Phasellus in arcu. Cras sem urna, gravida eget, facilisis a, vulputate eget, arcu. Quisque mi diam, cursus a, dapibus non, ornare nec, mi. Fusce et nunc vitae mi porta imperdiet. Etiam non quam. Pellentesque tortor. Duis vestibulum velit et lectus.

Someone said:

Lorem ipsum dolor sit amet, consectetuer adipiscing elit. Maecenas vulputate sodales dolor.

Someone said:

Lorem ipsum dolor sit amet, consectetuer adipiscing elit. Maecenas vulputate sodales dolor. Lorem ipsum dolor sit amet, consectetuer adipiscing elit. Phasellus in arcu. Cras sem urna, gravida eget, facilisis a, vulputate eget, arcu. Quisque mi diam, cursus a, dapibus!

Add a comment

Name:

Your web site (optional):

Message:

| Add comment |

At the top of the page is a clear site title followed by a summary. This is so users can gain some quick insight into what the site is about and what they can expect to gain from it.

The Obvious Blog

Short blog description goes here to provide context to users who land on this page and have no idea what they're looking at.

Search

In this site

A provocative post title goes here

Short summary of this post, so users can quickly determine if it's worth reading.

Lorem ipsum dolor sit amet, consectetuer adipiscing elit.

Subscribe

Next post
Some post title

Beneath that is the post title. This is shown using a large, serif font to contrast the small, sans serif font used in the body of the post (a trick commonly used in newspapers and on the Web to better visually separate titles from copy).

Since post titles don't always fully reveal the subject of a post (because, let's face it, *quirky* blog post titles are more interesting), the post title is followed by a short summary of the post. Users can now read a single snippet to determine whether or not the post is worth reading.

Next, of course, is the post itself, and the post is followed by a footer that offers the author's name and the date of the post.

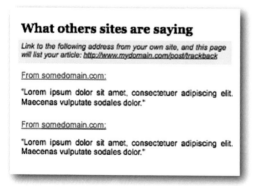

What others sites are saying

Link to the following address from your own site, and this page will list your article: http://www.mydomain.com/post/trackback

From somedomain.com:

"Lorem ipsum dolor sit amet, consectetuer adipiscing elit. Maecenas vulputate sodales dolor."

From somedomain.com:

"Lorem ipsum dolor sit amet, consectetuer adipiscing elit. Maecenas vulputate sodales dolor."

The next section is titled, "What Other Sites Are Saying." This section shows snippets from trackbacks, but in a way that explains to users where the snippets came from, along with instructions that simultaneously explain how to create a trackback and how they work. It states, simply:

"Link to the following address from your own site, and this page will list your article: http://www.mydomain.com/post/trackback"

With these instructions, a user can easily see how writing a post on his own site will result in a snippet displaying on the current page. Making it look easy encourages users to try it out. This not only encourages multisite conversation (for example, when someone writes a blog post in reaction to your post), it often results in increased traffic to your site as people reading posts on other sites click through to see the posts on your site that are referenced there.

Likewise, each trackback snippet features a link to the originating site, so users can click through to those posts and learn more about the subject or see what others think about it.

3 comments (Subscribe to comments)

Someone said:

Lorem ipsum dolor sit amet, consectetuer adipiscing elit. Maecenas vulputate sodales dolor. Lorem ipsum dolor sit amet, consectetuer adipiscing elit. Phasellus in arcu. Cras sem urna, gravida eget, facilisis a, vulputate eget, arcu. Quisque mi diam, cursus a, dapibus non, ornare nec, mi. Fusce et nunc vitae mi porta imperdiet. Etiam non quam. Pellentesque tortor. Duis vestibulum velit et lectus.

Someone said:

Lorem ipsum dolor sit amet, consectetuer adipiscing elit. Maecenas vulputate sodales dolor.

Someone said:

Lorem ipsum dolor sit amet, consectetuer adipiscing elit. Maecenas vulputate sodales dolor. Lorem ipsum dolor sit amet, consectetuer adipiscing elit. Phasellus in arcu. Cras sem urna, gravida eget, facilisis a, vulputate eget, arcu. Quisque mi diam, cursus a, dapibus!

Add a comment

Name:

Your web site (optional):

Message:

Add comment

Next is the Comments section, which is titled according to the current number of comments on the page. This heading also offers a link to subscribe to the comments of the post. (Very often, after writing a comment on a blog post, we like to see what other people say in reaction to it, but we forget to check back. With an RSS feed for comments, you can simply subscribe to comments and catch up on them next time you open your feed reader.)

Finally, there is a short form that enables users to add comments of their own. This further encourages conversation by asking only for pieces of information that will get used on the site—your name and Web address (which, of course, is optional). This is so your name can be displayed above your comment and it can be linked to your site if you have one. This means that writing a comment on a post can result in increased traffic on your own site. This further encourages people to contribute to the conversation.

Keeping the form as short and concise as possible means making the decision to comment a little more bearable. If it's easy and there's value in doing it, we'll do it. A short form helps make the decision easy.

In the left-hand sidebar of the design is a Search bar, followed by modules that link to other site sections, related posts, and popular posts. These link lists encourage users to read other posts on the site. Helping this even more is the module on the right side of the page that offers links to other post categories.

Also in the right-hand sidebar is a module for links to the next and previous posts, each of which is clearly labeled.

And finally, a large Subscribe button is featured at the top of the right-hand sidebar. The plain-English terminology and easy-to-spot button encourages users to take action and subscribe to the feed, or at least learn more about RSS via the information on your RSS-feed landing page.

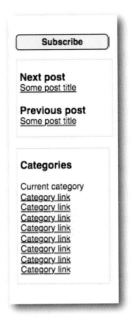

Follow not the fool

Sadly, as of this writing, I have not yet modified the design of my *own* blog to reflect these ideas, so who am I to tell you this is the way to go? But while I may have had exactly *none* of the typical design tools at my disposal when the idea for this blog template got started, I did have something pretty incredible on my side: three hundred people who were fanatic about blogging.

And the design discussed in this chapter is what *they* said should be done.

Corporate and professional blogging is still a fairly new idea, but the notion of speaking to your customers in an honest, down-to-earth voice is rapidly gaining traction as one of the best ways to tap into your audience's thoughts and opinions, and earn some of the precious customer loyalty afforded companies like Apple, Google, and 37signals.

And putting a little extra effort into your blog's design can make a big difference in your ability to connect with your users. Encouraging conversation through trackbacks and commenting, offering summaries of blog posts, and linking to relevant and related content are all surefire ways not only to improve your blog, but also to gain customer loyalty as a result.

One of these days, I hope to have the time to put these ideas to work on my own blog.

23

Inviting Discussion

The points I make in this chapter are not based on a single project. Instead, they are a mash-up of *almost every project* I've worked on that involved inviting users to add comments, write reviews, or participate in forum discussions.

See, whenever I am on a project like this, I invariably get asked the same question. It goes something like this.

> *We're considering whether or not we should moderate comments. What do you think about this?*

The driving factor hidden behind this question is, as you might guess, *fear*.

With regard to the user-generated content that results from such interactions, the fear is that someone will say something terrible that makes the organization look bad. Fear that someone will say something offensive to other users. Fear that internal staff will forget to look over the comments and make sure everyone is playing nice.

On the flip side of this is the fear that the staff will have to take on the ridiculously mundane job of marking comments for approval and deletion.

Next time someone asks me this question, I plan to refer them to this chapter, because right now, I'm going to tell you the same things I've told them.

▶ Letting Your Customers Speak

In short, don't moderate.

Don't moderate comments, reviews, forum threads, or anything else for that matter. Why not? Well, because moderation has one major negative side effect.

It can make your customers think you've got something to hide.

When we write a review for a product, for example, we believe that we're somehow helping another potential customer decide whether or not to invest in the product. Why else would we write the review?

Hence, if we have something positive to say, it means we're gleefully and willingly evangelizing a product the parent organization wants evangelized. This, obviously, is a good thing for the parent organization.

If we have something negative to report, however, we're trying to warn other users of issues we encountered ourselves. This is not usually malicious. Typically, we just want to relay some point of concern or difficulty so that others know about it in advance and aren't surprised by the same unfortunate circumstance. Yes, sometimes we want to wave giant red flags in the air and steer people as far away from a product as possible, but generally, products aren't so miserably bad that we resort to this.

If we write something up as a warning to others, and are told that our comments must be approved before they will appear on the site, we run the risk of losing a little bit of confidence in the site. Whether we're conscious of it or not, we wonder if the mighty moderators will stop our post from ever seeing the light of day. And let's face it, because of our busy lives, we're not very likely to check back on the site to see if the comment was added. When instant gratification dies, so does our interest. (Unless, of course, we have something really negative to say, in which case we might obsessively check back to make sure those pesky moderators approve the comment.)

And for all this doubt and wonder that we feel as a result of being held captive by moderators, the parent organization has almost nothing to gain from it.

In fact, since staff must waste precious minutes or hours to manage these comments, companies that do this are actually paying to lose their customers' trust.

Absurd, no?

A question of trust

There are several very good reasons to stop considering moderation entirely.

For starters, letting your customers speak freely shows that you trust them to talk about you. You trust them to evangelize your product when they have positive things to say, and you trust that their opinions mean something when they have something negative to say. And trust, as we all know, is the cornerstone of any successful relationship.

Next, it shows that you trust a user's ability to use his *own judgment*. Instead of shielding him from a negative reply to a forum discussion, you trust the user to leverage his own intelligence, common sense, and experience to filter through the negative, read between the lines, and generally make a decision for himself about whether or not a comment is worth considering.

In other words, give users the right to make their own decisions, and they will almost certainly ignore the useless comments on their own.

And if these reasons are not enough, you can use your customers' unfiltered voices to your advantage by tapping into your *otaku*.

Using your otaku

Otaku, as Wikipedia describes, is "a derisive term used to refer to 'people' with obsessive interests . . . ." (The term is generally applied to people interested in manga and anime, but marketing master Seth Godin's references to it in presentations and such have made it OK to apply it to other niches.)

The people who complain the loudest, cheer with the most fervor, provide the most help to people who needs questions answered, and are always around to tell you exactly what they think are your otaku. And you can use them.

By letting customers openly complain about your application, show their frustration in a forum post, or rant about something the company said on its blog, you give yourself the ability to see how people really feel. And an unfettered opinion is worth more than gold.

First, it's far better for someone to passionately hate your product than to have incited no passion whatsoever. The people who hate you the most can very often be turned into your biggest advocates the second you start heeding their complaints. If you manage to turn them around, you can earn lifelong friends instead of onetime screamers.

Second, you can shape the experience your customers have in these contexts by *organizing* it. You can, for example, contact a bunch of your most vocal and passionate users, tell them how much you appreciate their feedback and expertise, and ask them to become part of a team of volunteers who help out other users in the forums and answer questions.

In trade for this, you can offer them a direct line of communication with internal staff, discounts on licensing/subscription fees, send them free swag such as T-shirts and hats, and even offer to highlight them as community leaders on the site.

Adobe, for example, runs a program (of which I am currently a proud member) called Adobe Community Experts, or ACE. The ACE program is designed to reward active community members for their past advocacy of Adobe products. (These people are chosen not only because of their participation in forums, but also because they write articles and books, speak at conferences, and so on.) As a result of being invited into the program, members' bios are posted to Adobe.com, they are given images to post on their own sites so people know they are held in high regard by Adobe (which helps users trust the information on those sites more), and generally treated very well by Adobe staff. Inside knowledge, direct communication with Adobe product teams, and so on, are all benefits of the program.

Adobe does not pay these people. ACE members are volunteer experts. As such, they are one of the best advocate groups Adobe could possibly have. ACEs write articles, speak at conferences and user group meetings, and help out on forums.

The flip-side of this is that Adobe has equipped itself with a group of people who hang out on the forums all the time and answer questions, offer advice, and make recommendations. For users who think that unmoderated comments mean a company is *ignoring* the forums and that other users are ignoring their comments, this group of otaku is there to help out. They maintain an active presence in the Adobe forums and in user group discussion lists all over the world, and they serve on the front lines of customer service for Adobe. When negative comments come up, Adobe hears about them through the ACEs. When high praise comes up, Adobe hears about that, too.

Imagine if your company had such a group advocating your Web application and helping out the community at large. When these experts complain, you know there's some validity to it, and when they evangelize your applications, you know that other people can trust their opinions. *They do your marketing for you.*

Flagging the offenders

Finally, to quell any last concerns you may have, you can offer up a little piece of functionality that provides some of the safety of moderation with a lot less pain: a **flagging** feature.

Stick a small flag icon next to each review, comment, forum, post, and so on, that when clicked, offers users a way to mark the comment for review by staff.

This way, when a troll makes his way into your forums, other people can let you know they're annoyed by him and would like you to do something about it.

This flag icon should lead users to a simple form that lets them write in a message on why they think the content should be reviewed. Nothing more, nothing less. Keep it simple. And don't ask for anything you don't need (such as the user's email address, which you'd already have as a result of the user being signed in).

Get out of the way

So this, my friends, in so many words, is what I've told just about everyone who has asked me what I think about moderation.

You don't need to moderate.

Open up the floodgates, let your users speak freely, and get out of the way.

With a little humility and management, you can turn your customer base into a loyal and active community of fans and advocates. You can turn your fears into a tool for gathering information from your customers, developing otaku, providing superior customer service, and establishing a culture of trust between your organization and your users.

And doing so will win you far better and bigger rewards than any amount of moderation ever could.

24

Getting a Good Rating

Five-star–rating interfaces can be seen everywhere from Amazon to Yahoo to Yelp, but the individual implementations are often done very differently.

For example, they are often split into two parts, shown in two different areas of a page. One part is the **display** version of the five-star interface—the one that tells users the current rating. The other part is the **edit** version, where users choose how they want to rate something, such as a book, a CD, or an article.

Of these interfaces, some offer explanatory text that clarifies what each star means as a rating, and that appears alongside each star when the user rolls over the star with the mouse cursor. Some require that you click a star and hit Save. Some ask only that you click a star.

But when all you do is click a star, there is no feedback—no feeling of finality to the interaction—except that the star turns from white to yellow (or some other color). This design makes even me feel less confident that my action had an effect.

These are the issues I consider whenever I design a five-star–rating interaction.

In some cases, however, due to the limited page real estate, I also need to combine the two elements into one. I need a way to show the current rating and enable users to select a rating of their own all within a single interface control.

First, I'll show you how I do this now. Then I'll tell you how I was doing it wrong in the past.

▶ Clarity Over Efficiency

To combine the display and edit interfaces into a single piece, I split the display piece and the interactive piece into two states. I started with a simple display of the five stars, coupled with a link to begin the rating interaction.

☆☆☆☆☆ Rate this widget (Rated 14 times)

In order for a user to choose a rating, I decided the set of stars should go into an editable state when the user would click a **Rate this widget** link. When this happened, the stars would change from yellow to white.

Of course, the user also needs a way to save the rating and return to the display state, so the **Rate this widget** link is replaced with **Save** and **Cancel** options, which also indicate to the user that the widget is now editable.

☆☆☆☆☆ **Save** Cancel

So, the user simply clicks the **Rate this widget** link, then clicks the star she'd like to use to rate the widget.

☆☆☆☆☆ **Save** Cancel

At this point, she can click **Save**, **Cancel**, or another star. Let's assume she chooses to save the rating.

☆☆☆☆☆ Rate this widget (Rated 15 times)

Upon saving the selection, the average rating is updated and the new rating appears, again in the display state. Along with the word *Saved!,* this indicates to the user that the interaction is complete and her rating has been saved. This display state also offers a way to change the rating.

☆ ☆ ☆ ☆ ☆ **Saved!** (Rated 15 times) <u>Change your rating.</u>

I also put a little text next to the **Rate this widget** link that shows how many users have selected a rating. It reads, "(Rated 7 times)," (where the 7 is a variable number). This not only tells existing users how much stock they can put into the rating, but also tells the user that her rating has been added.

Finally, some logic is added to the interaction that prevents a single user from rating the same widget multiple times. That is, if she chooses a different rating on a future visit, the average is updated, but the number of reviewers does not change.

Combining the display and edit versions of a rating interface has its pros and cons.

On the upside, it takes less space than a two-piece version—you can find a single spot on the page for the component and move on.

On the downside, however, it takes several more clicks for users to complete this interaction than it does in other designs. But in this design—and this is my key point—each step in the interaction is explicit and clear.

As mentioned before, the two-piece version can be as simple as clicking a star, but it provides no feedback that your rating has been saved or that it had any effect. Combining the functionality into a single interface means that each and every step has a clear result.

Clicking **Rate this widget** makes the interface editable. Clicking a star changes it to yellow. Clicking Save lets you know the rating has been saved, updates the average rating, and updates the total number of ratings.

The interaction may take more steps, but it does a far better job of providing proper feedback, so users feel confident each moment they interact with the rating interface. It's clear at each step.

In other words, efficiency isn't always the answer to everything. As we saw with the insurance form in Chapter 16, shorter is not always better.

What matters more than efficiency is *clarity*. For users who are new to a site and/or are performing tasks they don't often perform, it's best to make each moment as understandable as possible. For users who are experienced with an application and/or are performing very common interactions, it's often best to shorten the sequence as much as possible so the process doesn't become annoying. In either case, what matters is that the steps are understandable and *appropriately complex*.

Because it is unlikely users will interact with a rating interface frequently enough to memorize how it works, and because they are faced with different versions on a many other sites, I erred on the side of clarity over efficiency.

Credit where it's due

I used to use this design without the "(Rated 7 times)" text, primarily because I simply didn't think of it. At the time, I thought I had taken the design far enough and talked about it during a presentation I was giving on *Designing the Obvious.*

During the session, an audience member suggested the interface should state how many people had rated the interface. This would help users get a better sense of how meaningful the rating was. After all, a five-star rating by one person doesn't necessarily mean the product is great, it just means that one person thought it was great.

A four-and-a-half–star rating based on 30 reviews, on the other hand, would be much more meaningful.

Standing there, I thought, Well, that's a jolly good point.

I said as much, and told the nice gentleman I'd be stealing his idea and using it in my next book.

So, here I am. Thanks, man.

PART VI

Managing Information

Almost every day, I burn up about two or three hours dealing with email, catching up on the news, reading blog posts, and checking out all the interesting links I learn about from those blog posts. That's two or three hours on a *good* day.

Clearly, I'm trying to manage too much information at once, but we'll save that conversation for another time. (And no, I don't count this as "professional development" time when billing clients.)

My point is that there is a huge amount of information online, and managing it can become a full-time job if we let it. The moments we spend navigating this data every day are aimed at achieving one major goal: to get organized, so we feel like we're active participants in our lives instead of stuck in rush hour trying to make up for lost time.

The same is true for the people who use our sites and applications. They have things to learn, plans to make, and all kinds of other things to do online. Whether they realize it or not, they're begging for effective methods to retrieve the information they want the most on a daily basis, and while there is plenty of technology to do it, most of the options have yet to break into the mainstream.

Even RSS—the solution many geeks live or die by when it comes to getting news and industry insights from trusted sources—has yet to become an understandable paradigm for information management en masse, let alone a household term.

So the next few chapters are about interfaces that facilitate the management of information. We'll take a look at ways to make foreign ideas such as RSS and tagging models meaningful, organize content within a page via a drag-and-drop interaction, and manage interruptions with system notifications.

We'll even talk about the notion of *designing for change* so that users can adapt to an idea before being dropped head-first into a potentially overwhelming design. (We have enough to think about. No need to keep piling it on!)

These moments are meant to be simple. Herein are some ways this goal can be achieved.

25

Making RSS Meaningful

One of the major difficulties in encouraging users to overcome the strangeness of a new Web technology and start taking advantage of it is in realizing that people don't care about the technology—they care about getting things done. Instead of selling technology, we need to sell the *benefits* of the technology.

To put this in context, consider RSS, which has failed to gain mass acceptance for a myriad of reasons. There's the potential difficulty of learning something new. There's the risk that the benefits of using a news reader aren't worth the effort of setting one up and incorporating it into your daily life. And there's the fact that most people—even some who are *already using a news reader*—have no idea what the term *RSS* means. The acronym is commonly used in buttons that go to subscription pages, but without knowing what RSS means, users are less likely to click these buttons. A button label, after all, should set a clear expectation in the user's mind about what will happen after clicking it.

When we promote a new technology, our first goal should be to make it approachable and understandable. People are more than willing to learn new ideas, but the ideas have to be learnable. This is true for *any* unfamiliar technology.

A few sites have attempted to help out on this front when it comes to RSS.

FeedBurner.com, for example, taught me a long time ago that the RSS subscription process doesn't have to resemble a visit to the dentist. Instead of showing a cold, ugly page full of XML and expecting users to understand automatically that they need to copy and paste the URL for the page into a reader application to complete the process, FeedBurner offered up something friendlier.

They showed me a reasonably attractive page with stylized blog posts. And while more and more RSS reader applications popped up online and for the desktop, FeedBurner offered up **chicklets**—one-click subscription buttons— with which I could subscribe to a feed with a single click. And while the acronym XML does show up on the page, FeedBurner avoided using too much technical jargon. *RSS* doesn't appear anywhere on the page.

Thanks, FeedBurner. I appreciate it.

AddThis.com offered something similar. They tossed a bunch of chicklets on a page and made it easy for anyone who already used a blog reader to subscribe. AddThis also almost entirely excluded the acronym *RSS* from the design, instead opting to refer to "feed readers."

These sites do a great job of making a foreign idea more approachable, but they are fairly exclusionary at the same time. They don't offer alternatives for subscribing to feeds—they focus only on subscription through an RSS reader.

Since there are more options, I decided to explore how the alternatives could be communicated and surfaced, so users could easily understand and use each one, and so the benefits of doing so are clear.

▶ Deciphering the Options

To complete my design, I started by using Subscribe as the label for buttons that lead to the subscription page, instead of RSS. Using terminology that supports a strong mental model can erase the language barrier and lower the learning curve for a new idea. Simple enough.

Then I picked up where FeedBurner left off: I created a section for chicklets. To avoid creating a new layout, I used the blog template I discussed in Chapter 22.

The idea here is that instead of sending a user to a FeedBurner or AddThis page, I'd show him a page that looks just like the rest of the site, retaining the block of site navigation and the Search field in the sidebar.

People who already have accounts with various Web-based or desktop reader applications can simply click a chicklet to subscribe with a single click.

For those who use feed readers not listed on the page, I added a method of simply copying and pasting the address for the feed into a feed reader, along with instructions about how to do so. In this field, the Web address is selected by default and the field is adjacent to a Copy button. This way, the user needs only to click Copy to be done with the page.

This addressed the first method of subscribing to a feed, so I focused on the alternative options.

First, I added an option for receiving email notifications about blog updates.

Several sites, including FeedBurner, let the user convert an RSS feed into an email newsletter subscription service. Since this is now such an easy and painless thing to do, we can offer the added functionality with little effort. In fact, providing the option to use email for content updates could even dramatically increase your subscription rates, as email is still one of the most effective methods of online marketing. (Not everyone reads blog posts—even when they have a reader account. People are much more likely to read their email.)

While making this design change, I also added the terms Option 1 and Option 2 to the headings. This is so users can, through deduction, quickly recognize that the first section is not the only option.

To address the last option—the ability to use a browser to subscribe to and read RSS feeds—I added a third section.

Subscribe to "The Obvious Blog"

This final section contains instructions for subscribing to an RSS feed using each of the major browsers (Internet Explorer, Safari, and Firefox).

Finally, to further address the main goal of making the technology more learnable, I replaced all instances of the term *RSS reader* with *news reader*.

Clear headings, simple instructions, and quick solutions already go a long way toward making the subscription process more understandable and worth trying out. Ditching the acronym RSS was simply a final attempt to make the technology more approachable.

With the three options of using a news reader, subscribing to email alerts, and using the browser itself to manage feeds, users now have plenty of ways to subscribe to the content, and each one requires very little effort. And by stripping out the geeky lingo, the whole idea becomes more understandable to people outside the tech industry.

Simply making a new idea learnable can be the key to its success or failure. Terms like *RSS* and *XML* get in the way of a user's ability to form a solid mental model and start reaping the benefits.

Get rid of them, and things become much more approachable.

26

Tagging It

Before I start ranting about the problems of tagging, you should understand something.

I really love the *idea* of tagging. Applying multiple tags to a single piece of content means increasing its findability and getting organized in a way that provides flexibility far above that of the folder-based organization method used by modern operating systems.

Using a tagging model, you can associate an email to topics like *work, to-do, this_week,* and *projects.* Then you can associate a research paper to *library, research,* and then to specific topics, such as *usability* and *user_experience.* And so on.

The flexibility of tagging means being able to find and organize content in myriad ways, all of which you can quickly define, in any manner that suits you.

Love it.

But tagging is not a perfect system all by itself. When you offer a tagging model to a community of users, things can get ugly fast. There are a bunch of potential problems.

First, much like RSS, tagging is a foreign idea, and few sites offer an interface that is self-evident and self-explanatory. Second, no one's native language includes terms separated by underscores, so the unfamiliarity of the jargon and syntax used in tagging models can lead to confusion about its usage. Third, because people are not robots, content is often tagged using multiple versions of the same tag. And finally, the search engines used by sites with tagging models often favor tags over more natural search terms.

| Everyone's Photos | ⬍ | voices that matter web design conference | **SEARCH** |

⦿ Full text   ◯ Tags only

For example, while hunting down images from the first "Voices That Matter" conference on **Flickr.com**, I ran a search for "Voices That Matter Web Design Conference." This is what I would search for using Google, so this is what I searched for using Flickr.

The Flickr search produced only four results.

I changed the search term to "Voices That Matter" and Flickr came up with over 700 photos. But about one-third of these were completely unrelated to the conference.

I added the word *conference* back into the search string, and this time came up with 58 results. I knew this was wrong, because I knew that one of the conference coordinators alone had posted more than 200 photos from the event.

Having run three versions of the most obvious search query and coming up with nothing, I decided to search using a tag. I entered *VTMWDC,* for "Voices That Matter: Web Design Conference" (the proper name of the conference). I got 294 results, and every single one of them was from the conference. Finally, a good search term.

Of course, I had no idea if this tag represented every image from the event. And I'm not sure how I was supposed to know to use the acronym for the conference as a search term in the first place.

If I hadn't imagined up my acronym search, I would have been stuck. But how can Flickr possibly expect me to know that searching by tag is more effective than by subject? And how am I supposed to know what tags to search for when looking for something specific? (I also searched for *VTM* all by itself and found some more images from the event.)

In order for a tagging solution to be truly effective, it needs to be accompanied by a few pieces of functionality that make creating and using tags easy and painless.

▶ Taxonomies, Folksonomies, and Anomalies

There are two different routes to take when deciding how to organize content on a site. One is to construct a **taxonomy**, which is a classification system you define once that is then used by everyone. The other is to enable a **folksonomy**, which is the collaborative version of a taxonomy. With this method, users can continually contribute to and change classifications to meet their needs.

When you make the decision to enable a folksonomy, using tags, all the aforementioned problems come right along with it. It's vital to design solutions that make the tagging model approachable to users, as well as support a strong mental model.

So when I designed a tagging model myself for the first time, I took all this into consideration and looked for solutions that improved the paradigms I'd seen.

Eliminating the language barrier

For starters, I tried to make the whole idea more approachable by taking away the technical jargon of "tagging," instead referring to tags as "labels," as is done in Google's Web-based email application, Gmail.

Labeling is an idea rooted in the physical world and is easily understandable by most people. We put labels on things all the time, whether it's a first name written on a box of leftovers from Chinese takeout or a sticker on a container of sugar that helps identify it in a cabinet full of ingredients.

Tagging, on the other hand, is not something we do in our daily lives. It's a new concept. As we saw with the acronym *RSS* in the previous chapter, using friendlier terminology can lower the learning curve for a new idea.

To further make tagging friendly and familiar, I decided that underscores should not be displayed or required to create phrases (for example, *my_house*).

Even if the system needed to save the tags using underscores (because tags were to be used to dynamically generate URLs on the site, which cannot contain spaces), they did not need to be shown to users this way. They can and should be shown using natural language.

Explaining new ideas

Next, I needed to make sure the purpose and usage of a tagging model was clear. I handled this by simply adding some instructive text. In other words, I attempted to *stop labeling the assumptions* (as described in Chapter 7) that users would know what tagging is and how it works, and tried to offer something short and concise that explained it.

This came in the form of a simple Help blurb that stated:

> **Label it!**
> *Make it easy to find your images by adding labels (e.g. "my house"). Apply as many labels as you like. We'll turn the labels into links, and you can simply click a link to see all the images using that label.*

Making suggestions

To address the fact that different people can, and invariably *will,* unknowingly create multiple versions of the same tag, we need a way to detect similarities and give users a way to choose an existing tag over a new one.

For example, a person uploading to a photo-sharing site images that all came from a Halloween party could label every image *halloween*. Another person from the same party could tag their images *halloween_party*. Both tags are perfectly appropriate, but since there are now multiple tags focused around the same idea—a high-level label for the event—other people at the party may be unable to find all the images with a single search.

(Incidentally, Yahoo! came up with a low-tech *preventative* solution to this problem during the South by Southwest Interactive conference in 2006. At the official Yahoo! party, signs were posted throughout the bar that instructed guests to label all their Flickr photos as *Yahoo!_bar_tab,* so that all attendees would be able to find them. This solution isn't sweeping the nation just yet, but it's interesting to imagine signs posted at every dinner, party, conference, and other event that tell people what tags should be used to document the event.)

I used a couple of different things to solve this problem.

First, I thought that the site should offer an auto-complete function like the one used by Google Suggest. As a user enters a tag, a search can be run for similar tags, and these tags can be displayed in a list so the user can choose the one that matches the best.

The potential downside to this, of course, as described in Chapter 9, is that she may choose a suggested tag over her own, even when her own might be better.

The second solution was to show a page of suggestions *after* the user enters her tags. Once the tags are entered, a search can be run for similar tags, which can then be presented as lists on a second page. The second page can explain in text that the user can match her new tags with ones that have already been created by other people.

This way, the odds of creating multiple versions of the same tag were reduced, making collections of related content easier to find.

Searching, searching, searching

Finally, the site's search function had to provide effective search results using more natural search terms instead of favoring tags (as with Flickr).

I'm not saying this would be an easy thing to accomplish from a development standpoint, but search is one of the most important pieces of functionality on most sites, and it's vital that it works well. If users couldn't find the content they wanted using the same natural language Google accepts, wading through information on the site would be a miserable pain in the neck.

The future of tagging

Again, foreign ideas need to be made learnable. The elimination of technical jargon *alone* would be an improvement on most sites that offer tagging, but obviously, the problem goes beyond the lingo.

Tagging is not something most people are familiar with, and as such, steps must be taken to help users form a clear understanding of how they work, find the content they want with very little effort, and organize content in ways that other users can easily find.

27

Getting Reorganized with Drag-and-Drop

One of the main selling points of an application designed to help you manage information is the ability to organize that information. With Dashboard HQ, users are able to create lists of links and personal notes and such, and are given complete control over what appears on the page. And since the content is 100% determined by the user, it's vital that the user be able to organize the information in whatever manner he deems appropriate for his needs.

To accomplish this goal, we offered up the ability to create and delete modules, write notes, add bookmarks, and so on. We also offered the ability to rearrange the modules using a drag-and-drop interaction, to enable users to get things in just the right order so everything can be easily found on return visits to the page.

But for drag-and-drop to be successful, the process needed to be clear and concise.

▶ The Three States of an Interaction

An effective drag-and-drop design needed to accommodate all three states of an interaction.

What are the three states, you ask?

Invitation

First, there's the invitation state. This state consists of whatever it is on the page that invites you to take action. This could be a button or a command link that triggers an action rather than simply loading a new page. Or it could be a tool tip that appears when you roll over an icon, or even a changed cursor, indicating that the user can take some action other than clicking.

Once a user clicks the Edit This Page link, putting the page into an editable mode, she sees the invitation states—the default state of almost any interaction—for several tasks. One option is to delete a module. Another is to rename a module. And the final option is to rearrange the modules via drag-and-drop.

The invitation state, then, is the word *drag,* which appears in the upper-left corner of each module.

Simple, no? All it does is invite the user to take action.

To complement this invitation, we display the *move* cursor anytime a user rolls over the word *drag.* This further communicates to the user that an action can be taken.

Manipulation

Second is the **manipulation** state, made up of the action a user must take to complete a task, however small it may be. This can be a single step, such as clicking a link to load a new page, or it can require multiple steps, such as copying and pasting the URL for an RSS feed into your favorite news reader and saving that URL to subscribe to the feed.

In Dashboard HQ, the manipulation state involves clicking the drag handle, dragging the module into a new position, and releasing the mouse button (or perhaps lifting the stylus) to "drop" the module into its new position.

Each step has to be as clear as possible for the user to easily learn and understand the interaction.

Now—to digress for a moment—this is vital to *all* interactions, regardless of its scope or purpose. All interactions need to be made as clear as possible.

I bring this up because I'm very often asked by people who have read *Designing the Obvious* what advice I might have for adapting the ideas in the book to more robust, enterprise-level applications.

My answer is always the same. Designing a large-scale application certainly means you have more to do, and more to think about, but *it doesn't change the rules.*

Large-scale applications still need to offer only the most relevant and essential features, use instructive design to get users up to speed, maintain consistency from one screen to the next, leverage design patterns to make interactions more learnable and repeatable, and so on. And each step of each interaction— particularly in the manipulation state—needs to be made as simple and clear as possible.

Not just simple. Not just clear. Simple *and* clear. (Sometimes this means requiring a larger number of simpler steps, as discussed in Chapter 16, while sometimes it means requiring very few steps for more common tasks.) If anything, this is *more* important in a large-scale application than it is in the relatively thin Web applications I often talk about. Bigger should not mean more complicated. Bigger should only mean, well, bigger.

Now back to the point.

Every step in the drag-and-drop interaction needed to make sense, whether a user was performing it for the first time or the 400th time.

So, once a user rolled over the drag handle, clicked, and started dragging the module, we needed to communicate exactly how the page would be affected by the change in position.

To do this, we created a dashed line that displays in the position where the module would be dropped, and we moved the other modules of out of their original spots to show exactly how each one would be affected by the move.

All that's needed to get through the manipulation state is to drag a module into a new position, but while doing so, the screen is updated as needed to show exactly how the manipulation will affect the page.

Completion

Third is the **completion** state. This is the one everyone forgets about. Believe me, I've done it myself. But perhaps due to an overwhelming need for closure, doing this invariably keeps me awake at night wondering why I'm not happy with a design. So I've learned my lesson and usually remember to account for it before it leads to a sleepless night.

The completion state is all about letting the user know that the interaction is, well, complete. Sounds ridiculously simple, I know, but it's one of the biggest reasons that poorly designed interactions *feel* poorly designed.

Sometimes completion means displaying an inline message that tells a user his profile information was saved. Sometimes it means showing a Thank You message after a user sends an email via a contact form. And sometimes it means sending a receipt and an update on shipping status after someone orders something through your e-commerce site.

Sometimes, though, the indicator of completion is less explicit. In the case of most drag-and-drop interactions, completion is indicated as soon as the module snaps into its new position and the other modules are snapped into their new positions right along with it.

This is how it works in Dashboard HQ. Nothing more was needed, and anything more would have overcomplicated the interaction.

The very common—almost innate—mental model of arranging papers on a desk or putting together a puzzle is quite enough to leverage with a drag-and-drop interaction, especially since people perform the same action with their operating systems almost every day while moving a file from one place to another.

Feeling complete

Regardless of the complexity of a single interaction, each of these three states needs to be represented so that users can figure out how to begin it, how to complete it, and then feel confident that they completed it correctly.

It can be very easy to forget all about the completion state—such as with five-star–rating interfaces in which you simply click a star and nothing else happens (as discussed in Chapter 24)—but without it, it can be very difficult for users to feel as though they've done things right and can move on with confidence.

No matter how simple or complex an application gets, each and every interaction can be made more effective by ensuring that each step is clear and that proper feedback is given along the way.

Justifying the functionality

Drag-and-drop interactions can be used in all kinds of great ways. On iGoogle and My Yahoo, users can rearrange modules on their personalized home pages. And on Ning.com, users can choose the elements they want to include in their social networks by dragging them onto a page thumbnail.

But even if they're designed well, drag-and-drop interactions and customizable home pages should be reserved for the right circumstances. They should be reserved for when the page containing the content is a *destination* instead of a gateway.

See, different applications play different roles. A project management system, for example, might be left open in a browser for days on end, continually being checked, updated, and reviewed. It's a destination. You're going to spend a lot of time there and, as such, will probably require a decent level of customization.

But a gateway is something you use on the way to something more important, perhaps only on occasion.

State government portals are a perfect example. You access a government portal site as a first step toward finding the thing you actually need, such as finding out how to renew your car registration online. A page like this does not require customization features, and in most cases, such functionality would be largely wasted, and can even make finding information *more* difficult instead of less.

When we hit pages like this, we scan them quickly, find the first link that looks reasonable, and get out of there as quickly as we can. This is not the kind of page we spend quality time tweaking and shaping to our specific needs.

Ironically, though, I often see gateway pages that have been turned into functionally rich, customizable home pages simply because someone at the organization thought that if it made sense for iGoogle, it would also make sense for them.

Imagine that your state government's Web site featured a three-column layout filled with drag-and-drop modules that enabled you to check the weather, get a current stock report, and maybe even play solitaire (all things you can do with iGoogle).

Strange, no? These are not the kinds of things people look for on a state government site, and a government would not benefit at all from offering this type of functionality to users. A site like this needs to remain focused on what users come there to find—information on government services.

Applications such as iGoogle, My Yahoo!, and Dashboard HQ, on the other hand, are designed *by* users, not *for* users. The content on these pages is determined entirely by the user, as though he is designing his own portal site—his own gateway. Because of this, these applications, which appear to be gateways, become destination applications.

I don't know about you, but I don't think I'm going to spend much time on the home page for my state government site regardless of how cool it is. And even if the employees use it as a homepage and would find customization features useful, this is an extremely small portion of the audience for the site. The site should not be designed for them—it needs to be designed for the largest chunk of their audience.

When it *does* make sense to provide such functionality, as with Dashboard HQ, it's vitally important that the interaction be fluid and enjoyable. Ensuring that all three states of an interaction are clear and obvious can go a long ways toward helping users to feel confident.

28

Managing Interruption with System Notifications

Let's say you work for a big ol' company about to release a major update to your most popular Web application. And let's say you've done all the design and development work, the application is now sitting in QA, and you're planning to flip the switch on the new version in a week.

And let's say you call me up at this very moment to do a usability review of the new design and you tell me all about your plan.

Wanna know what I'd say?

First, I'd say that next time you should give me more notice. But that's a different story.

Next, I'd ask if there was any way you could roll out an email to all your users, make a small change to the home page, and create a page that explains all the changes you're making. Then I'd ask if you could do it by the end of tomorrow.

That's right. I'm a slave driver.

The fact is, I've seen many Web applications go out the door with nary a word of warning to their most devoted users. You know, the ones that pay the bills and tell their friends. And when *those* users aren't warned about upcoming changes, then it's certain that the newcomers, who are still learning and deciding whether or not your application is worth using, aren't warned.

But there are some major advantages to telling your customers you're about to do something potentially disruptive to them. Here are the primary reasons to do this:

- It gives your most loyal customers something to get excited about and something to look forward to.

- It gives your most resistant users—the ones who hate when things change—ample warning, so they have some time to prepare themselves for the onslaught of new whizbang features.

- It gives you a chance to get people talking about the update before it goes live, so that your new version is welcomed with a huge amount of traffic and word-of-mouth chatter that gets you some new users.

- It prevents the shock of logging in one day to find out everything has moved or that a common task flow has changed. It lets people know they'll be facing a little reorientation soon, and that it will be worth the effort.

Sadly, many companies never even consider taking on the relatively small effort that's needed to reap all these benefits. I've personally fought to get companies I've worked for and with to make this kind of effort, but for various reasons they usually neglect to make any effort at all.

Sometimes it's because development teams are on skin-tight deadlines and simply don't have the time. Sometimes it's because marketing teams are afraid to let the cat out of the bag for fear that someone will come along and steal the idea before the release. (This argument is terrible, of course, because competition is a good thing, and it's far better to compete on merit than on how quickly you can get the update to market.) Sometimes it's because the powers that be simply don't see it as a high priority.

You know, because good customer service and a solid marketing effort aren't high priorities.

Ridiculous.

Our customers have loads of things to worry about in their lives, just as we do. Our job is not to surprise them one day with a new interface and expect them to drop everything and become an expert. Our job is to make their lives easier. If we warn them ahead of time, they can manage the information much more effectively than they could by being surprised on a random Tuesday morning.

▶ Designing for Change

So how do you design *for change*?

Answering this question means stepping away from what we normally think of as an interface and looking at the other ways we interface with customers. Outside the realm of check boxes and slider controls, we use all sorts of things we don't normally associate with user experience. Things like email, blogs, newsletters, screencasts, and screen-shot tours.

These things are all wonderful tools for staying in touch with our customers.

The first step in designing for change is to assess how the update will launch.

Will it launch on a specific date? If not, can one be set? Will the update affect all your customers or just a subset of them? Could the update benefit from some in-the-wild testing before it goes out to every last person who pays your bills?

Setting a specific date for the update to launch means you can give your customers exact information instead of surprising them with it one morning. Releasing the new version to a small percentage of your users before it becomes available to everyone else can give you some time to fix last-minute bugs. Telling your power users—the ones much more prone to discover hidden gems in the release than anyone else—about new advanced features can make your best and most loyal customers feel appreciated and that they're receiving special treatment.

Once you iron out how the release will occur, it's time to start telling people.

Start with a simple email. Send it to every last person who has registered for the application. The power users will gobble it up and tell their friends. Average users—likely your largest audience segment—will get ample warning that something is going to change soon. Users who have abandoned, but not deleted, their accounts—sometimes known as "sleepers"—will get a little nudge to check out your application one more time.

All it takes is a simple email, like this:

> *John,*
>
> *We'll be making a major update to* AcmeWidgets.com *on October 3rd.*
>
> *Now, you'll be able to:*
>
> - *Share your uploaded images with other people*
> - *Comment on images that you see*
> - *Contact members whose images you'd like to find out more about*
>
> *To see how this will look, cruise on over to* www.acmewidgets .com/update/tour.
>
> *The changes will be automatic—you don't need to do a thing. Just sign into the site on October 3rd as you normally do and start having fun.*
>
> *We thank you for your business, and we look forward to seeing what you do with AcmeWidgets!*
>
> *Sincerely,*
>
> *The AcmeWidgets development team*

Notification areas

Next, add something to the home page about the impending update. Some-thing simple and out-of-the-way, but still noticeable.

Here's a little trick I've used a few times, for notifications of various kinds. I call it the, um, *notification area*. (Genius, huh?)

You might recognize it from my personal site at rhjr.net.

Basically, it's a big black bar along the top of the page that contains a message, and it usually links off to another page with more information.

It's simple, clean, and effective. And that's exactly what you need it to be.

Which color you use is entirely up to you—just be sure it contrasts the other colors on the page so it gets noticed.

▶ Reusable Interface Elements

In *Designing the Obvious*, I talked about the use of Welcome screens to help users get up to speed with an application. I also mentioned that these elements could be reused to call out new features and the like later on, after beginning users have become intermediate users and no longer need up-to-speed aids.

This is the example I showed. No, it doesn't say Welcome. Its purpose is to intro-duce users to the page, it's positioned in the same spot Welcome text would typically be found, and it's meant for either instructive or marketing text.

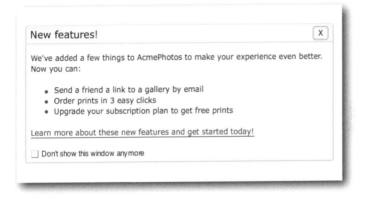

And this is how it can be repurposed to let users know about upcoming changes.

Simple, right? Users will already be familiar with the screen because they will have seen it during their first few visits. So popping it back into the screen will make it very noticeable and indicate to users that it probably contains important information.

Extending this idea, you can create a page that contains all the details about the site update and link to it from this screen or from a notification area.

The benefits of designing for change far outweigh the time and energy it takes to do so. These solutions are very simple, but they can have a major impact on how well your site update is received on launch day.

Whatever happens, don't surprise your customers with a major overhaul on some random Tuesday morning. Let them know what's going to happen so they can prepare for the changes, get excited about them, and start talking about your application again.

PART VII

Moving On

Saying goodbye is always sad in real life, but not so much when you're dealing with a Web application. It's all too easy to click that magic Log Out link (or Logout if you're at one of those sites I talked about in Chapter 3) and be on our way. And it's all too easy to simply never return.

The fact is, most people don't use Web applications for the sheer joy of it. They do so to get something done and get on with their lives. In other words, the primary goal for most people is to get *away* from a Web site. In fact, every chapter so far has been about how to enable people to get things done quickly, effectively, and with confidence, so that they can get away from the site. And the longer it takes, the less satisfied they can become.

But as designers, isn't it usually our goal to convince people to stick around a little while longer?

Well, yes. But this is not done by trapping people into complicated interactions and making things difficult. It's done by designing a series of enjoyable moments that make our users feel good about a product. So, ironically, the best way to get users to stick around is to help them get out as quickly and painlessly as possible.

So far, we've looked at how to make everything from page layouts to drag-and-drop interactions simple and effective. We've looked at ways to encourage users to explore a site, entice them to sign up, get them through complicated forms, teach them to use unfamiliar functionality, and even manage their data in the long term.

The last steps, then, are to explore what happens when they decide to leave the site, either temporarily or forever.

In this final part, we'll look at the sign-out process, how to encourage people to come back to a site after having been gone for a while, and how to handle account cancellations when they decide to bail out permanently.

Parting may be sweet sorrow, but when it comes to the design of interactions, even parting moments are an opportunity to make a lasting impression on a customer.

29
Signing Off

Signing out of a Web application is rarely a complicated task, but some sites make this far more complicated than it needs to be, and not enough sites take advantage of the opportunity that signing out presents to compel users to return.

More often than not, signing out entails simply clicking a command link in the upper corner of a Web page.

Such is the case with Blinksale, where you're simply returned to the Sign In page. This method is great for **closed systems**, when you are unable to see any part of an application without signing in. It's also the case with Scrapblog, where you're sent back to the home page for the site upon signing out. This is a good solution for **open systems**, when you are able to see some parts of the site without signing in.

Of course, not all sign-out processes are this clean.

▶ Complicating the Very Simple

LinkedIn, for example, makes you wonder if perhaps you're only halfway there. After clicking Sign Out, you see a page of text that explains the following:

> **You are now signed out.**
>
> *Your browser will remember who you are and you can still view your home page.*
>
> *To view or change your private information, however, you'll need to sign back in.*

This is followed by a button labeled Sign Out Completely and the instructions "when you click this button, this browser will not remember any information about you, and you will have to enter both email address and password to use the system."

No, I'm not kidding.

Aside from being a mouthful, these instructions can make you think you've done something wrong. Despite the fact that you've already clicked Sign Out, you now wonder if you're supposed to sign out *completely*.

Since we tend to look for buttons and links on pages and simultaneously ignore instructions, odds are that many people see that button and, well, get a little nervous. After seeing the button, you feel a little more like you *have* to read the instructions to figure out what's going on. If it wasn't for that button making us feel like our security is at risk, we likely wouldn't bother with the instructions at all.

In another example, we see the unnecessarily long model, such as the one offered by a banking site in Arizona. When you log out, you are shown a page that states:

> *Thank you for using the [Acme] Online Banking system! You have successfully logged out of the [Acme] system.*
>
> *To log back into [Acme] or to return to the [Acme] Web site, please click on the Back to Login button below. Otherwise, please close your browser window to end your session.*

This is followed by a Back to Login button.

Now, the log-in interface is on the home page for the site. So you access the site through the home page and you sign in from the home page, but when you sign out, you have to click a button to return to the home page. For no apparent reason.

And for some bizarre reason, the site designers decided you need two paragraphs of instructions to explain the Back to Login button! Even worse, the text is written under the assumption that a user will know what the cryptic phrase "end your session" means.

How can something so simple end up so complicated?

On top of this type of confusion, extremely few sites take advantage of the sign-out process as an opportunity for messaging or marketing.

▶ Compelling Users to Return

When I design sign-out processes, I almost always use either the closed-system sign-out or the open-system sign-out. But beyond this, I also like to find ways to encourage users to return to the site.

Gmail does a good job of this. When you sign out, you're returned to the Sign In page, but you're also presented with some information about features they'd like you to know more about. In this case, Google's sign-in page doubles as the home page for the application, and they simply used some of the extra space for marketing.

When I designed my own sign-out process for a closed system, I stole this idea. But I also wanted to expand on it. Sign-in/out pages in these systems are usually pretty empty, and it's more than possible to use the space as a marketing opportunity.

I started with a rather typical sign-in page, which is where users land when they sign out. It contained nothing but the user-name and password fields, an option to remember the user's log-in information, and a command link for retrieving a forgotten password. These elements were nested within a box that was centered on the page.

Next, I moved the whole thing over to the left and opened up a space for marketing copy. In doing this, I simply established a template that could be reused for whatever messaging a client wanted to use to communicate some of the benefits of using the application.

Reusing the space

Much like the Welcome screen discussed in Chapter 28, the marketing area of the Sign In page can also be reused to tell customers about new features.

To illustrate this, I created a second version of the wireframe.

To restrict the amount of text that can be put into the area, I decided to keep the marketing area fairly small—only about as large as the sign-in interface. This way, anyone who uses the area to advertise new or existing features, or anything else for that matter, would be confined to using bullet points and short statements to get their points across. (Remember, the longer the text, the less likely it will be read.)

Getting the message out

The sign-out process for a Web application can certainly be nothing more than a click followed by a return trip to the Sign In page, but with a little creativity, this typically empty page can be turned into a marketing opportunity.

It can be used to encourage users to return to the site by pointing out features they have not yet discovered; educate them about new features of events; and even announce an acquisition or some other bit of news that affects the entire customer base, such as a schedule maintenance outage.

And since the page contains nothing else, the text stands out more prominently than it would on a more crowded page elsewhere in the application.

30
Dusting Off Dusty Users

Dusty users, or sleepers, as 37signals calls them in its Signal vs. Noise post "Waking up the sleepers," are customers who signed up to use a Web application or service at some point, but have since all but abandoned the account. This happens when users get bored with a product, find an alternative they like better, or even just forget about an application.

I'm a dusty user for perhaps hundreds of Web applications right now. I'm sure you've got at least a few in your closet as well.

So what do we do about this as designers? If our goal is to keep users interested and engaged—which it is—what can we do to nudge these sleepers awake and get them moving again?

This is a question I really want to answer, but this type of design work is usually the job of marketing departments. Running promotions, advertising on television and online, offering coupons or other discounts—these are all the traditional avenues of promotion that are supposed to be enough to kick dusty users into gear.

But as good (or bad) of a job as marketing does at keeping a brand name fresh in our heads, it frequently does little to truly inspire us. The things that really make us pay attention are far more personal. They're not catch phrases screamed at us by roadside billboards, they're personal messages focused around our needs that create a genuine connection.

In other words, the job of waking up these sleepers is not necessarily only for marketers. It should also be the job of *designers*. After all, communicating and making connections with customers is what we do best.

To illustrate this point, I wrote a list of solutions for a hypothetical project, Acme Photos.

▶ Turning the Inactive into the Devoted

Many of the tools we need to dust off our dusty users already exist and are already being used in some other context.

For example, many of us already send out newsletters. While these are normally used to update customers on news and press about the company or to talk about new features, they have the added benefit of reminding dusty users that there's a good reason to return to the site and start using it again.

To optimize this effect, we can simply add a link to the newsletter email that encourages dusty users to explore what's new. We can also offer a discount or some other incentive to these users for inspiration. Here's an example:

> **Haven't used Acme Photos in a while?**
>
> *Let us convince you we're worth a second look! We've put together a collection of short and fun video tutorials about some of our best new features and put them all in one place, so you can quickly get up to speed and find out what we can do for you.*
>
> <u>Learn about our new features!</u>
>
> *And if that's not enough incentive, we'd like to extend a special offer. If the last time you signed into your account was over a month ago, we'll offer you a 50% discount on all merchandise through the end of February!*
>
> *Just enter this promotional code when you check out: FEB_PROMO*
>
> <u>Start shopping!</u>

By focusing on the needs of the dusty user specifically, and offering an incentive to give the site a second chance, we can appeal to the people who are wavering on whether or not they like a site and find it valuable.

Making it personal

Another option is to send personalized correspondence. For example, I recently received this snail-mail letter from a credit card company about an account I hadn't used in a while. It had a humorous tone and asked simply, "What have we done? (Or not done?)"

The whole point of the letter was to let me know the company noticed I hadn't used my card in a while and to encourage me to give them another shot. They apologized for not doing enough to make the card worth my while, and offered several upgrades to make sure I got the options I really needed from a credit card, such as travel and cash-back rewards, an increased credit limit, and paperless billing. And they stated that they were committed to doing whatever they could to make me an active card user again.

I really appreciated this, especially since I was in the midst of starting Miskeeto and needed a card for company expenses. Not only did I call to take advantage of some of the upgrade offers for my existing card, I applied for a business card at the same time. Since then, I've started regularly using both cards, and have become a good customer for the company. All because they sent me a letter that got my attention.

Here's an example translated to email form.

> *Dear Maggie,*
>
> *We noticed you haven't used Acme Photos in a while, and we're wondering what we did wrong. Are you seeing someone else? Do you just not love us anymore?*
>
> *We'd like a second chance!*
>
> *To prove our eternal devotion, we've created a collection of short and fun video tutorials about some of our best new features and put them all in one place, so you can quickly get up to speed and find out what we can do for you.*
>
> <u>**Learn about our new features!**</u>

And if that's not enough, we'd like to extend a special offer. We're offering you a 50% discount on all merchandise through the end of February!

Just enter this promotional code when you check out:
FEB_PROMO

<u>Start shopping!</u>

We're committed to making you a happy customer. If this email doesn't do the trick, please let us know what else we can do. By sending us a message through the form linked to here, you'll get in touch with a real person and have a real conversation about what else we can do to win you back.

<u>Talk to the Acme Photos staff!</u>

We hope to see you again soon. Really. We miss you.

Sincerely,

The Acme Photos team

As you can see, I played up the lost-love angle in this one. Humor can go a long way toward grabbing a user's attention.

Most important, the messages we send out should be written using a human voice, not with stiff, corporate marketing fluff filled with buzzwords and catch phrases. These messages should be conversational. They should be focused entirely on the recipient, not on us.

Of course, since both examples include links to a page of video tutorials, the next item on my list was to create a page of short and sweet screencasts. I talked about the use of video as an instructive aid in Chapter 8, so I won't go into those details again.

These things should help, but how do we determine why these dusty users got dusty in the first place?

Surveys

First, we can ask them why they've been gone so long. To handle this, we can add a survey to the list.

Using a service like SurveyMonkey, we can simply create a short survey asking customers how they feel about Acme Photos and send it out to the dusty users along with a coupon or some other promotional item as incentive to complete it.

The completion rate for such surveys will be undoubtedly low, but from the small percentage of people who do respond, it's possible to learn quite a bit about what's missing in the application or where it has disappointed these users.

From there, we can look at any trends that emerge and consider design changes based on that feedback.

But surveys aren't the end of the line. We can also, figuratively speaking, sit down for a drink with our users.

A chance to talk back

As the authors of *Cluetrain Manifesto* so aptly stated, "markets are conversations." But very few companies do a great job of actually listening to their customers and engaging in real conversations.

To get this conversation going, we can offer dusty users a chance to talk to a real team member to vocalize their concerns and wishes. This was promised in the email as well, so it's important to create a way to facilitate this.

This could be as simple as creating an email address to which users can send their comments with the promise that each and every email will get a response from a real person. But we can go way beyond this. For example, we can invite our dusty users to join a group focused on future improvements to the application.

These users can take part in a forum or discussion list with internal staff about what they'd like to see changed. For their time and energy, we can offer them discounts on subscription fees or other purchases.

To create a sense of exclusivity, we can limit the size of the group. We can form a group of, say, 100 users. We can send an email invitation to all the dusty users explaining the details of the group, and then tell them that only 100 people will be chosen.

Exclusivity breeds interest. Limiting the group to 100 people will make users feel like they're joining something special. It will also keep the group size down to a manageable number so that it is really useful to the company in the long run. And, of course, even the users who aren't selected for the group will understand that the company is taking steps to appeal more to its audience.

Don't overdo it

With all this in mind, the key to success is to avoid overdoing it.

If a user simply wants to be left alone, we can easily offend him by bugging him too much, and inadvertently force him to cancel an account he would rather have just let die on its own. We also don't want to sound desperate. So there need to be some rules in place.

The initial email that informs people of new features should be sent out once an account goes dusty for a relatively long time. If it's an application that would normally get used every day, this email should go out to users who have not signed in for at least a month. In the case of Acme Photos, where users sign in about once a week on average, the email should go out to users who go three months without signing in.

There is no mathematical equation here—just a hunch based on the frequency of use.

Beyond that, a more personal email, such as the example above, should be send out within a couple of weeks after the first email. This extra message should help further encourage users to get involved again while the first email is still in recent memory. If a user does nothing at this point, it's best to just leave her alone.

Now, as far as forming a group of dusty users goes, this can obviously be done only once or twice a year, with each group lasting perhaps a few months.

The email about the group can explain that it will last three or four months, and that a new group will be formed after that period is over. It can also explain that there is no obligation whatsoever for users to actively participate in the group, but that frequent participants will receive more offers for discounts and such.

If a group can be established and maintained twice per year, this email should go out a couple of weeks prior to posting the first discussion thread. The people who accept the invitation will spend this time getting re-engaged with the product, and maybe even mention to friends how great it is that the company is doing such a thing.

Between discounts, humorous messages, and a chance to communicate with real team members about the product, dusty users should have ample opportunity to get reinvested in the product.

In the end, it's all about good customer service. Every design decision, every conversation, blog post, comment, email, phone call, and so on—it's all about providing good customer service.

Do this, and you will earn loyalty.

31
Letting Them Go

Sadly, not everyone will love our work, no matter how good it is. Shocking, I know, but it's true. Even after we've done all we can to convince users to sign up, taught them to use the application through instructive and self-evident interaction design, provided loads of value, made data management as simple as possible, and even worked to dust off the dusty users, sometimes customers bail out once and for all.

And although this should be a sad moment, considered a mark in the Lose column, we usually have no idea when it happens. We don't have real-time alerts to tell us when someone has canceled an account. We don't look over their shoulders to witness the experiences that lead up to this fateful moment. To the contrary, this happens without our knowledge. All we see are the metrics that we collect to measure our progress, which reduce our customers—on whom our livelihoods depend—to little more than a series of numbers and charts.

Just like everything else in a Web application, our last-ditch efforts to retain a customer need to be automated so the system can do the work for us, while we sit at home watching *The Daily Show with Jon Stewart*.

And above all, we need to handle the situation gracefully. It may seem counterintuitive, but making it easy to abandon an account completely should be just as easy as everything else. But every application faces different challenges and has a different purpose and scope than others, so instead of telling a single story about account cancellations, I thought I'd tell you about instances from a collection of situations I've faced.

▶ Losing Gracefully

In every situation, I've avoided making a customer feel trapped at any point. I have no idea whether or not there is any science to validate this approach, but I very much believe it's the right thing to do.

Think about it.

A customer who feels locked into a service or subscription simply because there's no effective way to switch to something else will feel trapped. If that happens, she'll feel resentful, and resentment is one of the best ways to convince someone to say something bad about you. Also, if it looks like she'll be trapped at any point, she'll have incentive to bail out sooner than later. This lock-in strategy may work for cell phone service providers, but it doesn't fly on the Web.

Also, although we're losing the war to retain the customer, maintaining our dignity during this process is essential—not only so we avoid looking desperate, but also so that the customer has one last chance to be impressed by us.

So here's my advice.

Tying up loose ends

First, it's important to enable customers to tie up their loose ends. An application that a customer uses to manage all sorts of personal data, for example, must offer a way to retain that information upon cancellation, else the customer may never get involved in the first place.

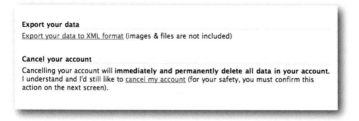

Backpack (created by 37signals), which offers users a way to organize small projects and collect content into a centralized location, does a good job of this by offering an Export Your Data feature on its Account page. Just click the link and an XML document containing all of the content from your Backpack pages will be created and emailed to you. And the fact that this feature exists on a very easy-to-access Account page, also used for upgrading or downgrading your subscription plan and setting other account information, means that you don't have to jump through any hoops to cancel your account. There are no hidden pages, no complicated steps. Within just a few clicks from any of your Backpack pages, you can export your data and cancel your account.

Knowing it's easy to cancel a Backpack account makes it very easy for someone to get invested in the application in the first place. The cost of switching—the time and money required to switch to another solution—remains low so that users feel comfortable using an application from the beginning.

Google Reader, a blog-reader application, offers a way to export your entire collection of RSS-feed URLs so that you can import it into another application and pick up right where you left off. Since many blog-reader applications offer a way to import such a list, it's very easy to explore several blog readers in a single day, trying each one out and moving on until you find one that suits you.

And in an application such as DropSend, an online file storage system, all you need to do is download any files you don't already have on your computer and you're free to cancel.

Gone, but (possibly) not lost

In each of these examples, the actual act of canceling is also very simple.

In Backpack, you can cancel an account in three clicks, using the **Account** link, the **Cancel My Account** link, and the "Yes, permanently cancel and delete my account" confirmation button.

Three clicks and you're out. Doesn't get much easier than that. Except, of course, for Google Reader.

In Google Reader you don't need to do a single thing. Because Google offers Single-Sign-On (SSO), enabling you to log into every Google application with a single user name and password, Reader is always available to you whether you use it or not—as are Google Calendar, Google Documents, and Gmail. If you want to use a different reader application, such as Bloglines, simply export your subscriptions as an OPML (Outline Processor Markup Language) file and import it into Bloglines.

In DropSend, simply click the My Account tab, the **Please Cancel My Account** link, and then the **Cancel my account and delete all files** confirmation link.

No matter what the application, it should be very easy for a customer to bail out. You've done everything you can to make the user's experience good up to this point in the application. The last thing you want to do is trick or force a customer to stick around when he doesn't want to. It doesn't help you, it doesn't help the customer, and it can result in the worst kind of word-of-mouth advertising—the kind where customers say bad things about you on their blogs and tell other people to stay away.

That said, you can certainly make one last attempt to dissuade a customer from leaving.

DropSend's cancellation process (for the free account, anyway) leads to a page that states:

Your DropSend account isn't costing you anything . . .

Are you sure you would like to cancel? You're on the Free DropSend Plan, which doesn't cost you a thing. Why not stay signed up, in case you need to send a large file or back something up to your DropSend Online Storage?

If your account is cancelled, all your files will be immediately and permanently deleted. This cannot be undone!

Cancel my account and delete all files

Back to my account

This message in unobtrusive, has a friendly tone, and might even do its job once in a while. As it points out, a person with a free account really has no reason to cancel when she can just as easily keep the account in case she needs it later on.

Another option is to send one last email to the customer upon cancellation. It could include something like this:

We're very sorry to see you go! We hope that your experience with Acme Photos was a good one, and we hope we haven't offended or inconvenienced you in any way.

If you're willing to give us one last chance, we'd love to tell you about some of our newest features and offer you a discount on your subscription.

Learn about the new features and apply your discount!

But if you're really set on leaving us, we hope you might take a moment to tell us why. It would really help us improve the site so we may win you back in the future.

Tell us what went wrong.

Thanks very much for your business. We appreciate it, and again, we're sorry to see you go. We wish you the best.

Without reeking of desperation, we can make one last appeal to a customer on his way out the door to stick around and give us another shot. No need to lose our dignity over it.

Losing gracefully is a very easy thing to do with a Web application, and the positive impressions we leave on our customers can far outlast the sting of losing a customer. Even a dissatisfied customer can be a source of positive feedback and word-of-mouth marketing if we treat them well.

All it takes it a little subtlety, respect, and professionalism when offering customers a way out.

The Keys to Great Design

In *Designing the Obvious*, I described seven core tenets of great Web application design and how to apply them to any project. I said, to design great applications, we need to:

- Build only what's absolutely necessary

- Quickly turn beginning users into intermediates

- Prevent errors whenever possible and handle the errors we cannot prevent gracefully

- Reduce and refine interactions and task flows until even the most complicated applications are clear and understandable

- Design to support a specific activity

- Make constant, incremental improvements to our processes and applications

- Ignore the demands of users and stick to a vision

These statements have guided me through project after project, proving to be an essential list of guidelines in which I strongly believe. With these guidelines, it's possible to achieve designs so easy to use that people attribute their ability to use them effectively to pure common sense.

And beyond these *macro-level* tenets, each user's experience with a Web application comprises a whole series of *individual moments*. These moments have a major impact on how a user relates to and perceives an application, and each and every moment needs to be designed. To achieve the best possible moments, we must also seek out solutions to the much more specific and individualistic design problems we face every day. Hence, in *Designing the Moment*, we've explored over thirty *micro-level* principles that can help you with everything from page layouts to social networking interactions.

But beneath all this lies a simple and basic truth. And every principle, concept, idea, and hunch I've discussed in this book and in *Designing the Obvious* is rooted in this single requirement that is the *absolute core* of any design project:

Design is *communication*. To design great experiences, we must be great communicators.

Communication Above All Else

Throughout this book, we've looked at ways to improve the moments that compose a user's experience with a Web application, from the first impression to the last, from the details of a drag-and-drop interaction to the disruption of a new release. We've explored principles and concepts that help support the ways human beings interact with Web applications. Help them analyze, judge, recover from mistakes, and stay on track after changing their minds or getting lost. Help them get oriented, form ideas, memorize, habituate, trust, get inspired, and feel productive.

As designers, we face a lot of challenges during the design of every interaction. We need to know how people interact online and what makes them love or hate an application. We need to know when and where to use which design patterns, understand best practices and current trends, know how to write well, and most of all, know how to make every detail of an application understandable so that our users can meet their goals and we, conversely, can meet our own.

To rise to this challenge, designers have come up with a huge number of variations on a huge variety of design processes and approaches, and have devised an enormous collection of design documents, flow charts, diagrams, and everything else you can imagine in an attempt to control the outcome.

What we've all learned, however, is that there is no magic bullet. There is no one way to design that works better than everything else. There is no single process to follow, no perfect design document, no giant tree of ideas from which to pluck moments of genius. We can change our processes a million times, switch up the types of documentation we use, and make any number of other changes to adjust and refine our ability to achieve success as we go along.

In the end, none of it matters one tiny bit. It doesn't matter how we achieve great design as long as we can repeat it. We can change our processes a million times, switch up the types of documentation we use, and make any number of other changes to adjust and refine our ability to achieve success as we go along.

But no matter what we do, our primary mission—to *communicate*—never changes.

We are communicators above all else. Whether designing an application, a slide deck for a presentation, a design document, or the drink counter in a restaurant, the goal is always to communicate to our users how something works, what they can get from it, and why it matters.

To do this, we communicate the purpose, benefit, and usage of an application and the interactions that comprise it through design patterns, instructive elements, and much more. We communicate emotion through color, imagery, and words. We communicate dedication to our users through customer service and quality product offerings.

We communicate all sorts of things all the time, whether we realize it or not. And when we communicate well, we earn respect and loyalty.

When we communicate poorly, however, we can earn the opposite. When we put out less-than-great designs, we communicate to our users that we're either less-than-capable or less-than-committed.

As designers, we have to put out designs that tell our customers we're 100% committed to making them happy, and that we're 100% committed to making sure they stick around and keep finding value in our products.

Applying the principles discussed in this book, and in *Designing the Obvious*, will go a long way towards helping you do exactly that.

But there's one last thing to understand, and it relates to the myth that good design is hard. That it's difficult to communicate well. That simplicity is really complexity that has been shifted from the front end—where users interact with it—to the back.

▶ It's Easier To Do It Right

Counterintuitively, it requires less thought or energy to communicate the right message than the wrong one.

Let me explain.

When I was 19 years old, I attended a *master class* with a friend of mine who was learning to play classical guitar. In a master class, a veteran "master" musician critiques the playing of student musicians and offers them advice and insights to help them improve.

The master, in this case, was a seasoned and worldly musician who played magnificently. The strings of his guitar seemed to sing every nuanced detail of the emotional content of the music. He was amazing. And my friend was no doubt a little nervous about being critiqued by him.

The nervousness translated for my friend into unusually tense hands.

The master noticed this. And when he critiqued my friend, he said something I'll never forget. He said:

> *Playing guitar badly is very hard. Playing guitar well is*
> *very easy.*

This statement baffled me. For years, I had no idea what he meant by it. He was like a shaman who had told me the greatest secret I could possibly know, but left me to my own devices to figure out its meaning.

Eventually, though, because I play drums myself, I came to understand what he meant.

When a guitarist plays well, it's because he's achieved a Zen-like calm. A *presence.* A *mindfulness.* His wrists are relaxed, his fingers are loose and ready to fluidly move from one point of the fretboard to the next, his breathing is steady. Instead of playing *at* the music, he's playing *in* the music. His whole soul exists in that moment only to be part of the very music that he is creating. It's a really beautiful experience, for both the player and the listener.

As a result of this wonderful, calm control he has over his playing, the guitarist is able to do more with less. Instead of cramming notes into every stanza, he lets the music breathe. Instead of constantly trying to demonstrate his dexterity and amazing skill, he knows that the notes he *doesn't* play are just as important as the ones he does.

He doesn't force everything he knows into the music. He *removes* as much as he lets in, if not more, because in music, the empty spaces give life to the full spaces.

The same is true in drumming, and in art, and basketball, and in Web application design (and much more).

It's far easier to use only a few words to communicate an instruction than it is to write a paragraph. It's far easier to build only the essential components of an application than it is to build all the bells and whistles we can think up. And it's far easier to create white space than it is to fill up every nook and cranny of an application screen.

In other words, it's far easier to leave things out than it is to cram them in.

It's far easier for a person to use an application that maintains these qualities than it is to use one that has become bloated from unnecessary features, complicated interactions, and snazzy interface gadgets that do more to show off a developer's skills than to serve their purpose.

Now, there is plenty of information available online from usability studies, tons of advice and information on design patterns and guidelines, and plenty of opportunity to seek advice from the experts through social networking sites and email. At this point in Web history, we've run out of excuses for bad design.

But most importantly, there's the simple fact that, as with my guitarist friend, it's *easier* to do something well than it is to do something badly.

To succeed, you need only to be mindful of your message and passionate about communicating it well. Everything else falls into place as a result.

By simply being mindful of your message, the goal becomes to see what is the least you can possibly do to accomplish this communication. More often than not, the *least* you can do is the right solution.

I hope that the stories I've told throughout *Designing the Moment* have helped you do exactly that.

Final note

Every one of us must carve our own paths and figure out what works for us as individuals. We must know ourselves—our limitations, our strengths, our pet peeves, our passions, and so on. We must pay attention to how we think and act, interact with colleagues and coworkers, and navigate difficult political situations. We must pay attention to how we design and seek out ways to make ourselves better, whether it comes from research, human observation, or just lots and lots of practice. We also must think about our environment, the tools we use to do our jobs, and how these things affect our ability to succeed. We must be mindful of all aspects of our lives in order to evolve as individuals.

Regardless of how you do it, what's important is that you remain mindful—in life, in work, and in design. Success will follow.

Good design, again, is the evolutionary result of a whole lot of bad design. Sometimes you get lucky on the first try. Most often, you don't. It's a long road. Stay on it—you'll find what you're looking for eventually. Keep moving forward, no matter what.

So that's my big advice.

Follow your bliss. Find your Zen. Design *your* moment.

*   *   *   *   *

To continue reading my thoughts on design, visit my blog at www.rhjr.net/theblog. To learn more about my company, Miskeeto, visit www.miskeeto.com.

Index

designing the obvious:
a common sense approach to web application design

Designing the Obvious belongs in the toolbox of every person charged with the design and development of Web-based software, from the CEO to the programming team. *Designing the Obvious* explores the character traits of great Web applications and uses them as guiding principles of application design so the end result of every project instills customer satisfaction and loyalty. These principles include building only what's necessary, getting users up to speed quickly, preventing and handling errors, and designing for the activity. *Designing the Obvious* offers practical advice about how to achieve the qualities of great Web-based applications and consistently and successfully reproduce them.

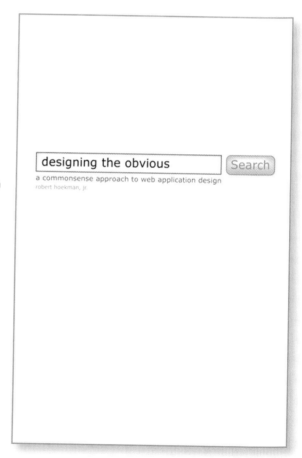

Robert Hoekman, Jr.
9780321453457, $39.99
264 pages, October 2006